Famous Stutterers

Famous Stutterers

Twelve inspiring people
who achieved great things while
struggling with an impediment

Gerald R. McDermott

 CASCADE *Books* • Eugene, Oregon

FAMOUS STUTTERERS
Twelve inspiring people who achieved great things while struggling with an impediment

Cascade Books
An Imprint of Wipf and Stock Publishers
199 W. 8th Ave., Suite 3
Eugene, OR 97401

www.wipfandstock.com

PAPERBACK ISBN: 978-1-4982-8229-1
HARDCOVER ISBN: 978-1-4982-8231-4
EBOOK ISBN: 978-1-4982-8230-7

Cataloguing-in-Publication data:

McDermott, Gerald R.

Famous stutterers : twelve inspiring people who achieved great things while struggling with an impediment / Gerald R. McDermott.

Description: Eugene, OR: Cascade Books, 2016

Includes bibliographical references.

Identifiers: ISBN 978-1-4982-8229-1 (paperback) | ISBN 978-1-4982-8231-4 (hardcover) | ISBN 978-1-4982-8230-7 (ebook)

Subjects: LCSH: Biography. | Speech disorders. | Communicative disorders.

Classification: RC424 M15 2016 (print) | RC424 (ebook)

Manufactured in the USA   OCTOBER 10, 2016

To Department Chairman Robert Benne and Dean Gerald Gibson,
who many years ago took a chance on a young professor
who stuttered

Table of Contents

Acknowledgements

For years I have kept lists of famous people who stuttered, and talked from time to time of sitting down and doing a book. My three sons kept urging me to "write that famous stutterers book, Dad!" Thank you, sons!

Thanks too to my wonderful wife Jean, who kept cheering me on and giving me clear directions on tone and method.

I am appreciative to many who read chapters and gave suggestions: Don Andre, Mark Graham, Bob Benne, Janet Thompson, Sam Cox, Matt Franck, Wilfred McClay, Dreama Poore, Ron Webster, Bill Fintel, Michael McClymond, Dikkon Eberhart, Elizabeth Haysom, and Judith Kuster.

This book would not have happened without the generosity of Byron Pitts, Annie Glenn, Peter Brown, and John Stossel—all of whom took time to invite me into their lives.

Finally, my editor Rodney Clapp was enthusiastic from the first day I told him abut this book, and gave me wise advice all along the way.

Introduction

In 2010 the movie *The King's Speech* took the world by storm. Winning four Academy Awards and seven British Academy Film Awards, the film depicted King George VI's painful struggle with stuttering. Its popularity was due to two factors. First, it was a gripping psychological drama revealing the king's inner frustrations and family conflicts, and tracing the efforts of Australian speech therapist Lionel Logue to tame the king's unruly tongue.

Second, most viewers were startled that such a well-known historical figure was afflicted with such a serious debility, and that he somehow found a way to give important speeches in a time of great crisis while England was at war with Hitler's Germany.

Just after my wife and I watched the film, a friend asked me if I enjoyed it.

"No, I suffered through it," I replied. "But it was a great movie."

I have been a stutterer since the age of six. Every time the king (Colin Firth) puffed his cheeks helplessly as he tried to get out a word, I felt his frustration and humiliation.

Most of us stutterers know all too well "Bertie's" fear of situations that would force us to read a text publicly or speak before a group. Most stutterers fear the telephone because we cannot control the dialogue. We remember painfully the innumerable occasions when we had all the right words in our heads but could not utter them. We groan as we think of all the well-meaning friends and family who told us—as they told the British king—to take a breath or just relax. If we could, we would!

Much of our agony is invisible. People who hear us block on words occasionally think it must be trivial, or a minor annoyance at most. But they don't know the times when occasional blocks mysteriously morph into paralysis, when even sounds that are normally effortless become mountains to climb. They have no idea of the apprehension when answering the phone, or the nervousness when, caught in conversation that goes quickly, we are afraid we won't be able to reply at the right pace, and all eyes will turn to us as the conversation suddenly stops. They don't know of the worry for weeks about upcoming speeches or presentations—not over *what* to say but *whether* we can get our tongue to cooperate.

Famous stutterers include Moses, Demosthenes, Churchill (whose problem the movie alludes to), Marilyn Monroe, Oral Roberts, Carly Simon, James Earl Jones, Tiger Woods, John Updike, Annie Glenn, and John Stossel. Eighty percent of all stutterers are males. It is estimated by specialists that roughly one percent of the population (3 million Americans) stutter, and that upwards of five percent (15 million) have stuttered at some time in their lives.

Like most stutterers, my disability started when I was very young. My mother feared I would flunk kindergarten because no one but her could understand me. Somehow I passed. But then in first grade my teacher put me in front of the class to help me enunciate. My panic developed into stuttering, which I would be helpless to manage for the next thirty-two years.

Stuttering often turned school into a nightmare. Fellow students looked at me quizzically and mockingly. In high school, one considerate lad asked me loudly why I could not talk like everyone else. I was glad to take Latin and Greek, so-called dead languages, because reading them was important—not speaking them. But I dreaded French class every day, when I would sweat rivers of living water down my sides as the recitation exercise made its way up and down the rows until it came to me. Everyone sighed because they knew I would take so much longer than everyone else, while I tried to force words from my uncooperative mouth.

In college I had to join in class discussion because the University of Chicago prided itself on small classes with lots of conversation. Sometimes, with the running start seen in *The King's Speech*, I might be fluent for a few sentences. But invariably I would grind to a halt, utterly tongue-tied before an intractable consonant.

I was humiliated when my grad school advisor recommended speech therapy. How did he know? Strangely, many of us stutterers are in denial. But the speech therapy I received there made no real attempt to cure me, instead trying to help me accept myself. It was a waste of time, at least for me.

Other speech therapists adopted something like the psychological theory used by the King's first therapist in the movie—thinking the cause of stuttering is childhood trauma. Attempts to help me talk through my supposed traumas did nothing for my speech. Later in life it dawned on me that many non-stutterers had childhood trauma, and many stutterers did not, or dealt with their traumas in healthy ways.

I wrote this book for a couple of reasons. The first is that the subject is fascinating. Most people are amazed that the famous people profiled in this book were bedeviled by such a difficult problem. For each, the ways it manifested were different, and the therapies they used to cope with it varied. But the fact that these great and famous people faced what could have been a debilitating problem and somehow accomplished great things anyway is intriguing. This fact surprises and gratifies most of us. We are surprised that they had a serious obstacle—and *this* obstacle in particular. We are gratified that their lives were not painless, for the thought that others can skate through life without serious problems would be unnerving for all of us who continue to struggle with serious problems.

The stories of the people in this book are inspiring. For all of these accomplished persons, stuttering was an enormous difficulty. None had a surefire remedy. Most had to blunder and stumble through. The persistence and courage they displayed tells us that there might be ways we too can survive and achieve—despite our own serious difficulties.

Malcolm Gladwell's recent book, *David and Goliath: Underdogs, Misfits, and the Art of Battling Giants* tells the story of cancer researchers, civil rights leaders, and other successful individuals who came from very difficult backgrounds. Most of his subjects suffered through traumatic childhoods or labored with disabilities and experienced deprivation and struggle. In fact, Gladwell suggests, these struggles were somehow instrumental to their later success. The stories of the famous stutterers in this book show that Gladwell's book might well be right.

This book looks at twelve of history's most famous stutterers. Many are surprises. Moses is one of the most important religious leaders of all time, a model in many ways for half the world's population—Jews, Christians, and Muslims. Few of his modern disciples, however, know that he probably stuttered. Yet it was an obstacle to his leadership from the very beginning of his work as leader for the Jews in Egypt.

Aristotle is one of the most important and influential philosophers in the history of the West. Scholars have known for a long time that he might have had a speech impediment. A close look at the evidence suggests that his impediment was not a lisp, as had been thought, but a stammer of some kind.

Demosthenes is the world's most famous stutterer. The story of his practicing at seaside with pebbles in his mouth is probably the best known story of speech therapy in history. Research, however, suggests that most of what history has said about this orator's speech defect was wrong.

Joshua Chamberlain was a college professor in Maine who volunteered to fight for the Union in America's Civil War. His key role in the battle of Gettysburg was first featured in the Pulitzer Prize-winning novel *The Killer Angels*, then made famous in Ken Burns's 1990 Civil War documentary, and immortalized by Hollywood in the 1993 film *Gettysburg*. None of these portrayals, however, revealed that Chamberlain had a horrible stutter over which he agonized in college, and had to fight to control the rest of his life.

King George VI's struggle is now well known. But what is not well known is that the conflict with his therapist Lionel Logue was manufactured by Hollywood (surprise, surprise), and that he got help from Logue long before the famous speech depicted in the movie. By that time, he had already been enjoying considerable fluency for ten years.

Winston Churchill's career is supremely ironic. Here is one of the world's greatest orators who had to struggle all his life against a complicated set of speech problems. Churchill never relaxed his vigilance against these handicaps, practicing his own techniques at great effort all the way through his career.

Marilyn Monroe was another stutterer. She spoke before a camera toward the end of her life about her teenage agonies with stuttering. Many have noted her breathy sexy voice. But no more than a handful have linked that slow and breathy voice to speech coaching she probably received in Hollywood to prevent the recurrence of her teenage impediment.

Peter Brown is one of the greatest historians alive. Most famous as a biographer of Saint Augustine of Hippo, the early Christian theologian, Brown is an Irishman who has taught at the world's most illustrious universities. He has written many books in the field of late antiquity and, in particular, the religious culture of the later Roman Empire and early medieval Europe. Most recently a professor at Princeton University, Brown has lectured all over the world. Yet he too is a stutterer, and the impediment still afflicts him today.

John Stossel is an American consumer reporter, investigative journalist, author, and libertarian columnist. In October 2009, Stossel left his long-time home at ABC News (anchor at *20/20*) to join the Fox Business Channel and Fox News Channel. Millions of Americans would be shocked to hear that this smoothly articulate journalist has ever had a problem with his speech. Yet Stossel reports that in his early days as a news reporter, he woke up every morning with fear of stuttering, and that while he no longer has that fear, he still lapses occasionally.

Annie Glenn is the wife of John Glenn, Ohio senator and first astronaut to orbit the earth. Annie was made famous by the movie *The Right Stuff*, in which President Lyndon Johnson rocks a white limo back and forth in rage in front of the Glenn house because

Annie won't come out of her house to face the TV cameras with him. He did not know that she had a severe stutter.

Byron Pitts is an African American TV journalist of some renown. Pitts could not read until he was eleven, and stuttered painfully until he was twenty. Since that time he has become an Emmy Award-winning journalist and correspondent for *60 Minutes*.

John Updike won two Pulitzer Prizes and scores of other awards, but is best known for his graphic but lyrical portrayal of the sexual infidelities of middle America in the 1960s and beyond. Many are unaware of his lifelong stutter that is strangely connected to both his own infidelities and his unique religious sensibility.

There is a red thread that winds through all the chapters that follow. It is red because red is the color of blood, and blood is a symbol of suffering. Each of these famous stutterers suffered greatly because of the gremlin that tied their tongues. Every one had thoughts to communicate and at times felt utterly unable to express those thoughts. Others thought they were stupid or unintelligent. Most were angry at themselves. Some hated themselves for it.

Some overcame the problem for the most part, even though all seemed to have known that stuttering rarely ever completely gives up its ghost. Others never attained mastery. Or, as they would put it, they found ways to cope and endure. Ways to speak somewhat more fluently, but without conquering the enemy. For them it was live and let live, and often a tense truce.

But for every one of these famous sufferers, a certain nobility emerged. From the war wounds came a kind of honor. They had engaged the enemy and did not retreat. Some were still the walking wounded. But they had persisted and come out on the other side. And through it all, they achieved other things in life. Things that mattered. Which is why they became famous, and we have their stories to tell.

Chapter 1

Heavy of tongue: Moses

In *The Ten Commandments* (1956), Cecil B. DeMille's epic film about the Jews' escape from slavery in Pharaoh's Egypt, the Moses played by Charlton Heston is strangely different from the Moses of the Bible. In DeMille's movie, Moses accepts without protest God's call to him to lead his people out of Egypt.

In the famous scene of the burning bush, the Moses of the movie asks, "Who am I that you should send me? How can I lead? What words should I use that they [his fellow Jews] will hear?"

God in the movie replies, "I will teach thee what thou would say. I will put my words in their hearts. Now go; I shall be with you."

In the very next scene Moses comes down from the mountain and tells his brother Aaron and sister Miriam, "He asked that I should go to Egypt." There is no hint that Moses was anything but completely and immediately obedient.

But in the biblical story Moses protests.

ARGUING WITH GOD

Moses was tending flocks for his father-in-law in Midian, which according to some scholars was in the northwest Arabian Peninsula, on the east shore of the Gulf of Aqaba on the Red Sea. He came to "Horeb, the mountain of God," and suddenly saw a burning bush—that kept on burning but miraculously did not disintegrate.

According to the biblical account, God spoke to Moses out of this bush, saying he had heard the Jews' cries for help and had seen their oppression. Now, the voice said, he had come to deliver them.

What then happened in the story shows several remarkable things. First, when this voice made promises, Moses seemed not to have believed them. In fact, he was stubbornly distrustful. Second, it was this conversation that suggested to the ages that Moses was a stutterer.

The voice promised he would send Moses to Pharaoh so that Moses could deliver his (God's) people.

Moses protested with a question. "How in the world could I deliver my people? That's impossible!"[1]

The voice tried to reassure Moses. "Don't worry. I will be with you. And here's my guarantee: after you have delivered them, you will serve me on this very mountain."

Moses probably wondered how that last promise was reassuring: I have to wait until after the deliverance to get a guarantee? That's hardly a guarantee!

So Moses demanded something up front. He asked what he could say or show to his people that would get them to believe that this God had indeed spoken to him. Moses asked, "Can you tell me your own special name?" (In the ancient world names were thought to reveal the inner identity of the human or divine person.)

The voice responded with a name that it had previously not revealed to any others of his chosen people—not even to Abraham, the father of the Jewish family. The voice said, "I am the God of Abraham, Isaac, and Jacob. My personal name is YHVH." (The last four letters mean, according to scholars, something like "Being Itself" or the "Cause of All That Exists." The Hebrew gives us only those four consonants; the usual English transliteration is "Yahweh.")

The voice went on to give Moses four more promises. God would deliver Israel (the collective name for the Jewish people) from slavery in Egypt, the elders of Israel would listen to Moses, Pharaoh would listen to Moses because of the miracles this voice would do, and this god would give Israel favor in the eyes of the Egyptians.

Moses still was unsure. He told the voice, "But the elders will neither listen nor believe me!"

DISBELIEF AND DISTRUST

The voice was patient. Even though, according to the story, Moses was in the presence of a continuing miracle—the burning bush— at this point God did not get angry. Instead, he tried to encourage Moses's faith by showing him several more miracles.

First he told Moses to throw down his staff. Moses did, and the staff turned into a writhing serpent. Then he told Moses to grab the serpent by the tail. Moses did, and it became a staff again.

There was more. The voice told Moses to put his hand inside his cloak. He did. When he took it out, the hand had become white with leprosy. Then Moses was told to put his hand back inside his cloak. When he took it out again, his hand was healthy once more.

Then the voice went even further to convince Moses: "If the elders don't believe you after these two signs, then do a third. Take water from the Nile and pour it on the ground, and it will become like blood."

But Moses was still unsure. Even if the elders could believe, he had no faith in himself.

"I am not eloquent," Moses told the voice. "I never have been. So I think you have asked the wrong man. For you see, I am *heavy of mouth and heavy of tongue.*"

Those last two phrases—*heavy of mouth and heavy of tongue*—are a literal translation of the Hebrew.[2] Most commentators have taken them to refer to stuttering. Moses was saying that he could never lead his people out of slavery, even if this god did miracles, because he could not speak without stuttering.

Most stutterers would sympathize. They know that "heavy" feeling. They too would never imagine they could do the public speaking that is necessary to lead a nation. Think of the agony that faced King George VI in the movie *The King's Speech* as he contemplated having to ascend the throne.

Once more the voice was patient with Moses. It sounded like a father who sends his terrified son on a walk in the woods at night, and reassures him that he will follow close behind. The son doesn't want to listen and stubbornly refuses to go. So the father must become emphatic.

"Who do you think made you this way, Moses? Who makes anyone mute or deaf or blind? Is it not I, YHVH? Don't you think I know what I am doing?

"Now go! I will help you speak without stuttering, and I'll even tell you what to say—word by word, thought by thought."

Moses was still unpersuaded. "I'm sorry, my Lord. Can't you send someone else?"

Now God got angry. Apparently he realized there was no more use trying to move this stubborn, untrusting man Moses. So Yahweh devised, we might say, Plan B. "OK, if you won't lead by yourself, I will use your brother Aaron as a spokesman. He'll be glad to do it (unlike you!). So you will tell him what I tell you, and I will help both of you as you work as a team. Aaron will be your mouth, and you will represent me to him. Take your staff with you, because you will need it for the miracles I will do through you."

Moses took the staff and the voice did ten spectacular miracles through him. The last—slaying all the firstborn animals and sons of Egypt—was what finally persuaded Pharaoh to let Moses's people go.

SURPRISES AND LESSONS

The story, then, is full of surprises. Moses, perhaps the greatest biblical character in the whole Hebrew Bible, was stubbornly distrustful of Yahweh. The God of the Bible, surprisingly, tolerated Moses's unbelief and stubbornness. He used Moses anyway—despite Moses's unbelief and despite Moses's speech defect. He overcame Moses's unbelief by forgiving him and by showing his own divine stubbornness, we might add, by staying with this stubborn human being. YHVH overcame Moses's stuttering by using Aaron, his brother. Another surprise is that Yahweh said he was ultimately responsible, in some mysterious way, for all defects, including stuttering.

There are fascinating lessons in the Moses story. One which we will see again in this book is that a very important person in world history was a stutterer. He never seems to have been cured of his stuttering (more on that in a bit). He was ashamed of his stuttering, and was handicapped by it. He made excuses because of it, and tried to avoid his life calling because of the fear his stuttering inspired. Yet, according to the biblical story, history pushed him into that role anyway. He wound up fulfilling that life calling, despite his stutter.

WAS IT REALLY STUTTERING?

There are other lessons. But first let us ask if we have over-interpreted this short passage about Moses's speech. Was it really stuttering?

Some of the rabbis, who wrote about this story for centuries in Jewish books called *Mishnah* and *Talmud*, didn't think so. The eleventh-century rabbi Abraham Ibn Izra thought Moses had a speech impediment, but not stuttering. The rabbi wrote that Moses could not produce all the normal sounds with his tongue and lips.

Two centuries later rabbi Bahye ben Asher got more specific: Moses was unable to pronounce the "z," "s," "sh," and "ts" sounds. More interestingly, he explained why. Moses was a beautiful boy (the Bible says he was "fine/beautiful" in Exodus 2:2), and one time reached for Pharaoh's crown when the two were together. Pharaoh's counselors thought that was a bad sign, and advised the king to kill the boy. Others suggested a test. So they brought a golden bowl and bright glowing coals, to see which he would try to touch. According to the rabbi, an angel guided Moses's hand to the coals, to show Pharaoh that this boy was not a threat. The boy

Moses then stuck his scorched fingers in his mouth, which dam-aged his tongue.

Other Jewish interpreters thought the Hebrew phrase "heavy of tongue and mouth" meant that Moses's speech was just fine, in fact eloquent. Some said it meant he spoke slowly and carefully, without the glibness characteristic of frivolous persons. A first-century Aramaic translator said the Hebrew word for "heavy" really meant "deep," so that Moses was profound in his speech. An-other rabbinic interpreter said that Moses was not tongue-tied but humble, recognizing that his brother Aaron was a better speaker.

Still others have thought that Moses's problem was linguistic. According to Sigmund Freud, Moses was Egyptian and could not speak Hebrew. Other historians have suggested that Moses knew both languages but spoke Hebrew with a heavy accent.

But the majority of commentators down through the ages have considered the fuller story and concluded that the text does indeed mean that Moses stuttered. The eleventh-century rabbi Rashi, the most popular of all Jewish biblical interpreters, insisted that Moses was a stutterer. He and others have pointed to the story about Moses speaking to the two "Hebrews" who were fighting, and engaging one of them in a conversation (Exod 2: 11–14) as proof that Moses knew Hebrew and could be understood by his fellow Jews.

The nineteenth-century rabbi Samson Raphael Hirsch ex-plained that another passage in the Exodus story describes Moses as "uncircumcised of lips," and that the word for "uncircumcised" here means "unpliant" or "without control over the faculty denot-ed." In this case, the faculty is "lips." Hirsch, who was a renowned specialist in the Hebrew language, said that this meant Moses did not have control over his lips, which is exactly how stutterers feel about their lips.

A contemporary interpreter, Samuel Davidkin, says that an-other passage in the story provides still more evidence. Exodus 6:9 says that when Moses spoke to the Israelites they did not listen to him "because of shortness of breath and hard work." Most inter-preters have thought this referred to the overworked Jewish slaves, but it may refer to Moses himself. For a stutterer, speaking a long message (and in this case it *was* long) before a crowd can be exhausting, and often means the stutterer runs out of air repeatedly while he speaks. Davidkin thinks the crowd might have run out of patience with Moses as they watched him struggling to get words out of his mouth.[3]

Most Jews have accepted this basic line of interpretation—that Moses was a stutterer. One piece of evidence for this acceptance is a modern joke whose impetus was the puzzling fact that the Jews got the only land in the Middle East without oil (though more recently natural gas reserves have been discovered off the coast of Israel). According to the joke, God offered Moses his pick of lands. Moses somehow knew that Canada possesses an enormous variety of natural resources, including oil, and so tried to get the word out. But when he stammered, "Can-Can-Can . . ." God thought he was saying "Canaan," and rewarded him with what we now know as Israel.

MODERN EVIDENCE?

In a recent issue of the journal *Neurological Science*, three medical researchers have suggested even more evidence. They say that the Moses story betrays three tell-tale symptoms of stuttering—fear, finding someone else to speak as a spokesman, and the pattern of negation/hesitation/avoidance. More intriguingly, they point out that Moses's father married his own father's sister (Exod 6:20), and that there is a higher prevalence of speech disorders among today's Israeli children born from consanguineous (same blood) marriages. They also find that stuttering today is more prevalent among bilinguals (those who speak two languages), and that Moses probably had to master three languages—Hebrew (taught by his parents in his first years), Egyptian (learned during his thirty-plus years as a foster son of Pharaoh's daughter in the royal household), and Midianite (learned during his forty years as a shepherd and husband to the daughter of the priest of Midian).[4]

Even more intriguing is their second piece of evidence, that Moses found someone to speak for him. Actually the biblical text has God saying, "I will be with your mouth and with his [Aaron's] mouth" (Exod 4:15), which suggests "choral speaking"—the two brothers speaking at the same time. This is plausible because most stutterers speak fluently when they read or speak the same words with another person. The biblical story even seems to indicate that Moses might have grown in his self-confidence after a period of time of choral speaking with Aaron. After Exodus 5 Moses speaks with Aaron only occasionally, and after Exodus 10:3 he seems to go it alone.[5]

These are of course circumstantial lines of evidence, not direct proof. But they are suggestive and confirming—that what most interpreters over the millennia have concluded is supported by patterns we see among stutterers today. The Moses of the Bible, from evidence we see in the biblical story, seems to have been a stutterer.

SENSORY TRICKS

But did Moses continue to stutter after this divine encounter? There is no sign in the biblical story that his stuttering ever abated. Quite the contrary—there is evidence that it continued because of hints that he developed coping mechanisms.

The three researchers we just discussed think Moses used two "sensory tricks" to help him get his words out.[6] They point to evidence that some ancients might have used staffs as therapy for stuttering, just as stutterers today sometimes stamp their feet to get a word out. The "rod of God" that reappears several times in the Moses story (Exod 4:17 and Num 20:9, e.g.) might have been a "sensory trick" to help him get over obstacles in his speech. Another trick that is familiar to many stutterers today is singing. Almost all stutterers find that they can sing words which in regular speech they find impossible to pronounce. Interestingly, Moses sang some of his longest utterances in the Bible (Exod 15:1; Deut 31:30, 32:44).

TRAUMATIC CHILDHOOD

Down through the ages it has sometimes been asked why Moses protested so much at the burning bush. Why could he not trust God when he was in the presence of a miracle? After all, if a bush could keep burning without being consumed, why could this stutterer not trust God to do what might be considered a minor miracle—heal his stuttering?

If we take the biblical story at face value, we can see some connections between the story of his earlier life and his refusal to believe at the burning bush. We can infer that his reluctance to trust the deity probably started with almost being killed at birth. This was in what most scholars say was the thirteenth century BCE, when Jews were slaves in Egypt, and Egypt was the superpower of the Ancient Near East. Pharaoh, the king of Egypt, was afraid that his Jewish slaves were multiplying so fast that they might overwhelm their Egyptian captors. So, according to the biblical story, he gave an order to the Jewish midwives to kill all male Jewish babies.

But the midwives slyly and courageously evaded the royal edict, telling Pharaoh that the Jewish babies came too quickly for the midwives to intervene. Apparently their tale was believed. Moses's mother was able to keep Moses secretly at home for three months, but then realized she needed to do something else to keep him from being seen and perhaps killed by the Pharaoh's soldiers.

So, not unlike mothers in recent centuries who have left their babies on the steps of an orphanage, Moses's mother put her son in a basket of bulrushes, daubed it with pitch for waterproofing, and placed it among the reeds by the riverbank. She sent her daughter to keep watch. Pharaoh's daughter, who was bathing that day in the Nile, saw the basket and heard the baby crying. She felt sorry for the little boy. Before she could decide what to do, Moses's sister called out to Pharaoh's daughter, "Shall I get one of the Hebrew women to nurse the baby for you?"

Pharaoh's daughter agreed, and paid Moses's mother to nurse her own son. When Moses was weaned, the sad day came when he had to be returned to Pharaoh's daughter, and raised in the royal palace.

So after being raised for five or more years by his own parents, and no doubt taught both the Hebrew language and religion, he was yanked away to live in a new and strange place, with strange people in a strange culture with a strange language.

How traumatic! Little Moses must have felt deep pain and confusion, perhaps even rejection, as many children feel when their parents give them up to someone else. No matter what parents say to explain, displaced children often wonder what they did wrong to deserve this. They suspect their parents don't love them—for if they did, they would not let their children be taken away.

Moses might have wondered why the Jewish God—whom his parents probably said loved the Jewish people—let this terrible thing happen. How could this be love? Taking him away from his parents? How could this God be trusted? Perhaps he spoke the word "love" but didn't really mean it.

MISUNDERSTOOD AND UNAPPRECIATED

The Bible says that when Moses was older—Jewish tradition in the New Testament says he was forty—he came upon an Egyptian beating a Jew. Looking this way and that, Moses struck the Egyptian and killed him. He hid the body in the sand. The next day he came upon two Jews fighting and asked the one in the wrong, "Why did you hit your friend?"

"Who are you to judge me?" came the reply. "Are you going to kill me just like the Egyptian you killed yesterday?"

Suddenly Moses realized his killing was known, and he might be in danger. But he also realized that his effort to help one of his own people was unappreciated—even after saving a fellow Jew from possible death! Once again, he must have wondered: did the Jewish God care about the people he said he loved? His parents had taught him that four hundred years before, this God had led the whole clan down to Egypt, rescuing them from famine and prospering them. But then when a new Pharaoh arose who did not know their ancestor Joseph, the Jews were forced to become slaves.

This was love? Could this God be trusted?

Pharaoh heard of the killing and sent men to kill Moses. So he fled—far away to Midian, in what is now western Saudi Arabia, about 370 miles to the east. There too he showed he had an instinct for helping people in trouble. When he first arrived, the seven daughters of the priest of Midian were trying to give water to their father's flocks when shepherds came and drove them away. Moses intervened. The Bible says he "stood up and saved them."[7]

LONELINESS AND EXILE

According to tradition, Moses lived in Midian for forty years as a shepherd. These must have been lonely years. Even though he had a Midianite wife and son, Moses was far from his own people and language and culture. He named his son "Gershom," a word that sounds like the Hebrew word for "sojourner," as a reminder that he was a stranger in yet another strange land. He was also far from the attractions of learned civilization, in the skills of which he had been trained in Pharaoh's household. During these long years of exile, he must have wondered why he had been given a great education—only to stare at the desert by day and the stars by night while tending flocks. He might also have wondered what ever became of the God who said he had chosen Moses's people.

It was at this point that he came upon the burning bush. When the voice from the bush told him that he could lead his people—slaves with no weapons—away from the world's superpower of the day, and that God would enable him to speak fluently enough to do so, he might have felt he had good reason not to trust this Jewish God.

DID STUTTERING CHANGE MOSES?

Let's conclude this chapter with a reflection on how stuttering might have affected, or even changed, Moses. As we have seen, it might have made it hard for him to trust the voice coming from the burning bush. He might have blamed this deity for not helping him or the Israelites generally during their hard times in Egypt. Later on, however, after seeing repeated miracles to help the Israelites escape from slavery and then survive for forty years in the Sinai desert, Moses became a different man. He seemed to trust the God of Israel when others did not, and came to an intimacy with this deity that no one else enjoyed in biblical history. According to the Bible, Yahweh said that he spoke to Moses face to face—or, literally, "mouth to mouth." Moses could see the Lord's "form" (Num 12:8), which was described elsewhere as the "back side" of God's "glory" (Exod 33:23). So it may be that the stubborn distrust which stuttering helped induce in Moses was somewhat or largely evaporated by his years of experience with this God in the exodus and wilderness wanderings.

But if the physical handicap of stuttering helped create a spiritual handicap in Moses, it might have also helped deepen his character. In the biblical story Moses is called the most humble man on the earth (Num 12:3). When his authority was challenged by others, as it often was, he typically chose not to scream in retaliation or strike out physically. Instead, he withdrew to prayer. Sometimes the Bible says the God of Israel did a miracle to reinforce Moses's authority, and at other times this God struck directly against those making the challenges. But Moses apparently did not tend to defend himself when challenged. That is a sure sign of what we would call meekness or humility today.

COMPASSION AND COURAGE

How could stuttering have played a role in that meekness? Its continued presence might have reminded him of his earlier disbelief and distrust in the divine voice, which had since that time proven its commitment to both Moses and Israel. In other words, it would have reminded him of his earlier distrust—his persistent refusal to accept the divine promises, even when being shown (according to the story) miracle after miracle.

This might have contributed to his extraordinary compassion for people. Twice when this God got angry at the people of Israel and threatened to wipe them out and start all over with Moses, Moses pleaded with Yahweh to spare the people. Other leaders might have taken YHVH up on that offer—especially after their people had rebelled against their leadership, as the Israelites often rebelled against Moses's leadership. But Moses had compassion on his rebellious people, and pleaded with Yahweh not to destroy Israel (Exod 32–33). We can guess, with good reason, that Moses's memory of his own kind of distrust, triggered in part by his stuttering, caused him to commiserate with his fellow Israelites.

Living with stuttering takes courage. Moses chose to continue in leadership for forty years, even though his stuttering must have caused continual strain. Aaron could not have been at his side continually as spokesman, for Aaron became high priest and had his own tasks to perform. The Bible claims that throughout those forty years Moses decided court cases as chief judge, at first all the cases of all the people, and then only the hardest cases (Exod 18). He must have pronounced his judgments on his own most of the time. Not to mention all the other innumerable decisions and statements—prophetic, political, military, economic—required of the leader of a people numbering 600,000 men and so perhaps 2–3 million people overall.

It took courage to continue to speak with a speech impediment. The courage he learned as a speaker might have helped him be courageous as a leader generally. For courage in one area of life often inspires courage in other areas. And the biblical Moses was nothing if not courageous. He stood up against the leader of the world's only superpower, Egypt, defying him repeatedly, even while being threatened with destruction. He stood up against rebels from among his own people, and remained strong amidst all the trials of the wilderness over forty long years. When he commissioned his successor Joshua, his most basic instruction was, "Be strong and courageous" (Deut 31:6).

Moses's stuttering might have been like a toxin that causes pain in a body. In the best-case scenario, the body develops antibodies to attack and disable the toxin before it kills the body. In Moses's case, the antibodies were the coping mechanisms he developed to help him continue as leader even with this handicap. They prevented the toxin from killing his leadership.

They might have also had side effects, as antibodies often do. For example, the body reacts to the stress of exercise by secreting antibodies known as endorphins. A side effect of endorphins is a pleasant sense of well-being, sometimes called a "runner's high." In Moses's case, the side effects to the antibodies he used to help him struggle with the toxin of stuttering might well have been greater meekness, compassion, and courage.

In other words, we have reason to believe that stuttering helped make the biblical Moses a better person. He did not let stuttering cripple him, even though he was tempted to do so. By his struggling with it, he became a bigger man.

Chapter 2

Hindered in speech: Aristotle

Aristotle (384–322 BCE). The name is intimidating. He is widely regarded as either the greatest mind or one of the two greatest minds (the other being Plato, his teacher) in the ancient world. The greatest philosopher of the Middle Ages, Thomas Aquinas, re-ferred to Aristotle as simply "*the* Philosopher." His influence upon the history of western civilization has been vast. It would not be off the mark to say that our own world would be very different if this man with very thin legs and small eyes had never raised his voice to teach students about the nature of the world and humanity.[8]

Strangely, this beautiful mind was intimidated by his own speech. Or so it seems. His ancient biographer, Diogenes Laertius, wrote that Aristotle had a speech defect. More on that below. Aristotle himself went to surprising lengths describing the intricate workings of speech defects, suggesting to readers that he was intimately acquainted with the frustration and pain they produce.

A FAILURE OF POWER

Stuttering, Aristotle wrote, is "an inability to express oneself continuously . . . as the derivation of the word shows." He was referring to the Greek root, *ischō*, which means "to check or restrain or hinder." This restraint on the tongue results in "less control . . . a failure of power . . . difficulty . . . hindrance . . . [and] paralysis."

Sometimes it is exacerbated by "nervousness" and "fear." It tends to make stutterers "melancholic." At times they "pant" because they run out of breath. At other times they make "a violent effort" and "speak in a louder voice" to get their words out.⁹

Stutterers, according to the Greek philosopher, sometimes feel that their tongues are "chilled" and thus cannot move as smoothly as they would like. At such times a glass of wine can help, for "wine which is naturally hot dissolves this chilling effect." The result is that their tongues seem to be able to move more smoothly: "When heated by wine and by continuous talking they connect their words more easily."¹⁰

Aristotle was also familiar with another phenomenon most stutterers experience—their thoughts running far faster than their tongues. The philosopher connected this with the melancholic disposition he thought was common to stammerers (a word which Aristotle translators used as a synonym for stutterers): "Why are stammerers melancholic? Is it because melancholy is due to following the imagination quickly, and this is a characteristic of stammerers? For the impulse to speak precedes the capacity to do so, as the mind is following the image too quickly."¹¹

The Greek thinker sketched accurately the problem nearly all stutterers experience on a regular basis—hurrying to get a word out before they block on a sound, and as a result running out of breath. "Why do men stammer? Is it because they are too hurried owing to the heat, so that they stumble and hesitate, just as men do when they are angry? For these too are full of short breathing. . . . Or do they pant because of the boiling of the heat" that builds up because of the pressure on their lungs? Aristotle compared this shortness of breath to the quick breathing of "men who are angry."¹²

UTTERING THE SAME SOUND FOR A LONG TIME

His more detailed description of stuttering was so precise that many stutterers today would say "Here is a man who understands!" This is his report: "[Stutterers] utter the same sound for a long time, not being able to make the next one, as the movement and the lung travel in the same direction owing to the quantity and force of the breath." In another analysis, he wrote that stutterers tend to move quickly with their speech in one direction, as it were, and find it nearly impossible to change direction—to produce a different kind of sound. He compared this to men running violently: "It is difficult to change the whole body from a movement in one direction to a movement in another."[13]

THE VOICE OF EXPERIENCE?

Whom was Aristotle talking about? Others? Or himself? In other words, was Aristotle simply a keen student of this human phenomenon, just as he carefully studied thousands of other phenomena in the human and natural worlds? Or were these observations remarkably penetrating because they came from his own experience?

If his ancient biographer was right, they came in part from his own experience. In his *Life of Aristotle*, Diogenes writes that Aristotle was *traulos tēn phōnēn*—"[H]e spoke with a lisp." This is how R. D. Hicks translated the Greek in 1925 for the Loeb Classical Library.[14]

At first glance, it would seem that Aristotle's speech defect was a lisp rather than a stutter. For Aristotle himself made a distinction between the two, and used the same Greek word for lisp which Diogenes used to describe Aristotle's speech problem.

But there are reasons to question Hicks's translation of Diogenes. For one thing, the key Greek word (*traulos*) seems to have been a general catchall word for speech impediment. The most respected Greek Lexicon of ancient Greek literature, published in 1996 by Clarendon Press in Oxford, defines *traulos* as "mispronouncing letters, lisping, stammering."[15] It also tells us that the Latin word for this same phenomenon was *balbus*, which was onomatopoeic (sounds like what it means) for "speech defect, stammering, lisping."[16] If it truly was onomatopoeic, then it sounds more like stuttering than lisping. Stutterers often repeat the beginnings of words that start with consonants like "b," as in "b-b-b-ball."

This is why *balbus* sounds more like stuttering. People who lisp have no trouble saying a "b" or any other word that starts with a hard consonant; their difficulty is with pronouncing an "s" or "z" or "th" clearly. Not repetition but clarity. So when Diogenes wrote that Aristotle was *traulos* in his speech, he might have meant simply that Aristotle had a speech defect of some kind, or that he was a stutterer.

A further piece of evidence is what Aristotle himself wrote about speech defects. He did indeed use *traulos* for lisping, another word (*ischnophōnoi*) for stutterers, and described both lisping and stuttering with a precision that sparkles today. But he wrote far more about stuttering than lisping. And his description of the emotional and physical trauma involved with speech defects was applied almost entirely to stutterers, not lispers.

A DISFLUENT TEACHER

So why did Professor Hicks, who was at Cambridge University when his translation of Diogenes was published in 1925, choose to say that Aristotle's problem was a lisp instead of a stutter? We cannot say with any certainty. Perhaps he thought that a stutter would have made it impossible for Aristotle to teach, and we know that Aristotle taught at Plato's Academy in Athens, and at his own Lyceum in the same city—besides spending some time tutoring the future Alexander the Great.[17] Yet we also know that other teachers have been stutterers, even some great ones such as Albert Einstein and the contemporary Augustine scholar Peter Brown.

We should also note that Diogenes wrote his biography roughly six centuries or more after Aristotle died. Historians are skeptical of many of the details in his *Lives of the Philosophers*. So he probably was passing on accumulated legend about a speech defect in Aristotle, perhaps without specifying what kind it was. Since Aristotle used *traulos* only for lisping, and Oxford's *Greek Lexicon* of ancient Greek says that *traulos* came to mean both lisping and stuttering, the meaning of the word could have changed between the times of Aristotle and Diogenes. It might have changed from a more precise meaning (lisping) to a more general one (speech defect)—just as "leverage" was once used only for a wedge in the work of ironworkers and carpenters, but is now used more generally for ways to open up relationships, futures, and whole lives.[18]

The bottom line: we don't know for sure what kind of speech defect Aristotle suffered from, but he does seem to have struggled with some kind of hindrance when he spoke. Yet his own writing on speech problems, because it focuses far more on stuttering than on lisping—not to mention the internal pain he seems to have known—suggests that he was a stutterer.

DEALING WITH FEAR

Which brings us to the payoff, or what we can learn from Aristotle. Really, it is what we can learn from all these famous stutterers: stuttering did not stop them from achieving great things. But Aristotle's achievement is all the more remarkable for two reasons. First, his profession was more involved with speaking than that of some others in this book. And second, ancient philosophy depended far more on speaking than modern philosophy does.

Today you can write a book, and if it is successful, change the world without speaking a word. A philosopher can gain fame and influence people simply by writing on a computer, without ever opening her mouth. This presumes of course that the philosopher's book sells!

But there was no printing press in the ancient world, and scrolls were very expensive to make. So few people had them or read them. Although Aristotle apparently wrote out some works in full, all of them have been lost. The only Aristotle texts we have today were compiled by his students from notes they took while

Aristotle was lecturing in public. This means that the power for which Aristotle is known—and which was responsible for influencing a great part of the Western world—came from spoken lectures. This despite a speech impediment that was probably a stutter.

If we are inferring rightly—that Aristotle's speech defect was a stutter—we can also infer that he struggled through these lectures. For he writes with telling exactitude of the paralysis, fear, and sometime melancholy that stutterers feel.

This suggests something else about Aristotle in particular and perhaps stutterers in general. There might be a link between the courage they muster to speak in public (some of course avoid this like the plague) and courage in other areas of life. Aristotle showed courage by breaking with his master Plato in some important respects. We need not detain ourselves with the specifics of these important philosophical differences, but suffice it to say that Aristotle brought philosophy down to earth from its Platonic obsession with eternal "Forms" beyond this world. This took courage. When he returned to Athens in 335 after tutoring the young Alexander the Great, Plato's Academy was flourishing under a new director. Aristotle boldly set up a new school of his own, the Lyceum. Perhaps the courage Aristotle nurtured by a lifelong struggle with stuttering spilled over into other kinds of public boldness. Or perhaps the two sorts of courage mutually strengthened one another. We cannot say that things work this way for all stutterers, but we do know that public speech requires courage for all stammerers—which means that if they persist in public speaking, they learn things about courage that can carry over into other situations.

More broadly, there might be a lesson for the rest of the population that struggles with problems and handicaps other than stuttering. All of us have some nemesis that inspires fear, melancholy, and sometimes emotional paralysis. Perhaps we can be encouraged that one of the world's greatest philosophers did not let that fear—perhaps even panic at times—keep him from forging ahead.

Chapter 3

The stutterer who wasn't: Demosthenes

Oddly, Demosthenes (384–322 BCE) was an exact contemporary of Aristotle. Both were born and died in the same years. Surely they knew of each other, for the two were both leaders in the city-state of Athens, which had only about 30,000 adult male citizens. But we have no plausible record of any contact between the two. This may have been partly because of their different political sympathies. Aristotle came from northern Greece, near Macedonia, and both he and his father worked for kings of Macedon—Aristotle's father served as court physician to King Amyntas, and Aristotle was hired by Philip II to tutor his son Alexander. Demosthenes is known for his lifelong antipathy to Macedon and its kings because of what he thought to be their threat to the freedom of Athenian democracy.

"THE PERFECT ORATOR"

While Aristotle was the most dominant philosopher of the period, Demosthenes was its most famous and effective political leader. He was effective because of his celebrated oratory. Quinitilian, the ancient teacher of rhetoric, said Demosthenes was *lex orandi* (the standard of oratory). Cicero said he "stands alone among all the orators. . . . [H]e is the perfect orator" who lacks nothing. Demosthenes's oratory and technique were imitated by figures as diverse as the authors of the Federalist Papers, major orators of the French Revolution, Henry Clay, Friedrich Nietzsche, and French Prime Minister Georges Clemenceau.

THE MOST FAMOUS STUTTERER?

Demosthenes is also the most famous stutterer of the ancient world. Outside of Jewish circles, Moses's stuttering has not been well known. Nor has Aristotle's speech defect been well known or well understood. But Demosthenes's supposed stuttering is often claimed to be the best example we have of this malady from the ancient world. For example, in a recent otherwise-excellent review of stuttering treatments in history, Benson Bobrick claims that Demosthenes was "possibly the most famous stutterer who ever lived."[19]

But was he a stutterer? The evidence we have suggests he was not.

Let me explain.

Our best source for the actual details of Demosthenes's life is the brilliant social history of the ancient world written by Plutarch, a Roman historian at the beginning of the second century CE. In his *Lives* Plutarch wrote that Demosthenes did indeed have a speech impediment, and that Demosthenes—in a story that has been repeated for almost two thousand years—was helped to overcome it by bellowing speeches out with pebbles in his mouth while walking along the ocean.[20]

"INARTICULATE"

On a first reading of Plutarch, one might gather that this world-class orator, whose speeches Queen Elizabeth studied in Greek in order to strengthen her own orations, stuttered. For Plutarch wrote that an old man Demetrius "the Phalerian" said he was informed by Demosthenes himself that "his inarticulate and stammering pronunciation he overcame and rendered more distinct by speaking with pebbles in his mouth." Plutarch also referred to Demosthenes's "shortness of breath," which stutterers often experience when trying to get too many words out on one breath.

But the first clue that this might not have been stuttering is Plutarch's using the words "inarticulate" and "rendered more distinct." These words suggest the problem was not getting words out but pronouncing them clearly. And shortness of breath can be caused by things other than stuttering. I have seen students huffing and puffing when they recite speeches that have long and complex sentences and they are nervous to start with. Or others, who do not stammer, become short-winded when they are simply nervous or worked up emotionally.

"SICKLY" AND "DELICATE"

There are other clues. Plutarch says that Demosthenes, who lost his father at the age of seven, was sheltered by his mother. She would not let him get out much, which either caused or exacerbated a "sickly" and "delicate" constitution. This too could cause shortness of breath in an inexperienced and nervous speaker.

Furthermore, at the age of twenty Demosthenes argued his own suit in court against his legal guardians who had been stealing his inheritance. Plutarch tells us that the young man's victory in this suit (although he never got back all the money) gave him "confidence" in speaking. As a result, Plutarch explains, Demosthenes ventured into public speaking before large audiences in Athens.

Now this was *before* he used the pebbles and undertook other strict training to improve his speech. It is highly unlikely that at this point, while still stuttering, he would have gained confidence from speaking in court, and so much so that he would want to speak before large groups.

But venture forth he did, and Demosthenes fell flat on his face. "When he first addressed himself to the people, [he] met with great discouragements, and was derided for his strange and uncouth *style*." I italicized the last word to emphasize what it is not. In other words, Plutarch does not tell us that the cause of

Demosthenes's discouragement was his stammering, but his style. He specifies this style: it was "cumbered with long sentences and tortured with formal arguments to a most harsh and disagreeable excess." His indistinct pronunciation and shortness of breath resulted in "breaking and disjointing his sentences," which in turn "obscured the sense and meaning of what he spoke."

In other words, this amateur speaker was trying too hard to be intellectual, making complex arguments with long and convoluted sentences. That doesn't work today, and it didn't work in ancient Athens.

DICTION LIKE PERICLES

An old man named Eunomus apparently had heard him give this amateurish speech, noted his dejection afterwards, and went up to encourage him. Plutarch tells us the old man told Demosthenes that no matter what other shortcomings, he nevertheless had the diction of Pericles, another legendary orator.

This is another clue that Demosthenes's problem was not stuttering. Stutterers are almost never praised for their diction because their labored and violent attempts to push out sounds so distract their hearers that good diction on their unblocked words goes unnoticed.

The old man told Demosthenes that his problems were cowardice and a weak spirit. Even in times when little was known about the causes of stuttering, people knew that cowardice and lack of effort could not be causes. They saw as well as we can see today that most stutterers put too *much* effort into pronunciation, and that this excessive effort contributes to blocking on words.

Plutarch tells us that on another occasion when the crowd refused to listen to Demosthenes, and he was dejected again, an actor friend suggested a way to get people to listen. The solution this actor, Satyrus, gave him had nothing to do with enunciation or pronunciation, which one would expect if the problem was stuttering. Instead Satyrus tutored Demosthenes in how to express the "proper mien and gesture." He said that effectiveness comes from the right facial expressions and body language, plus raising and lowering one's voice for effect. Once again we see that the advice proffered had nothing to do with getting words out without blocking. Telling a stutterer to move his body and face and volume differently is about as helpful as suggesting that someone blind squint his eyes to let in the right light. The supposed solution does not help.

PRACTICING IN A CAVE

No, Demosthenes's problem had something to do with lack of determination. For Plutarch tells us that Demosthenes set out with Herculean discipline to remedy that. He pulled out all the stops to "exercise his voice." First he dug out a cave into which he would retreat every day for two or three months to practice speeches. He would make up speeches based on conversations he had had in the street. Or he would hear speeches in the Athenian assembly, and come back to the cave to correct them, making what he felt were helpful changes. Then he would deliver them to himself over and over. To make sure he was not tempted to quit, he shaved half of his head, reasoning that the embarrassment of showing himself in public would keep him in the cave practicing.

To strengthen his voice, Demosthenes gave speeches to himself while running, or when climbing a hill. This was the time when he would go to the beach and declaim against the roar of the waves while stones rattled in his mouth.

All of this suggests that Demosthenes's speech problem was not stuttering. It seems to have been partly a problem of sophomoric writing—using tortured sentences and unexciting reasoning—and partly having a weak constitution and voice. These he treated with rigorous discipline and exercise.

RHOTACISM

But there is also good evidence for a third problem—an inability to pronounce the "r" sound. In Demosthenes's speech "On the Crown," which the *Encyclopedia Britannica* has called "the greatest speech of the greatest orator in the world," Demosthenes refers to a nickname he was given in childhood, "*Battalos*." Plutarch thought this meant "having the appearance of being sickly and meager." But Harvey Yunis, a scholarly expert on Demosthenes, argues that by the time Plutarch wrote (more than four centuries later) the original meaning of the word had been lost. "*Battalos*" originally referred to rhotacism, which is mispronouncing an "r" as an "l." Yunis adds that English "has no common name for one who suffers from rhotacism; 'lisper' or 'stammerer' is the best expedient."[21] This is why the Modern Library edition of Plutarch's *Lives* refers to Demosthenes's "stammering pronunciation."[22]

This would also explain why rigorous discipline could help. Forcing oneself to articulate a sound properly, and then to do it automatically on a regular basis, would take thousands of repetitions in order to produce new muscle memory. Speech therapists know this today. Demosthenes's story is evidence that it worked for him.

Rhotacism also helps explain why Demosthenes's problem was said to be a problem of articulation. This is not the way stuttering would be described. Stutterers block and stammer and start and stop, full of frustration and exasperation, sometimes violently and with contortions. Proper articulation, or pronouncing words in precisely the right way, is not the problem for stutterers. Their problem is being able to get *any* articulation out of the word *at all*.

NOT A STUTTERER, BUT . . .

So Demosthenes, perhaps the world's best-known stutterer, was probably not a stutterer after all. But his story is still an important one for a book on famous stutterers. Since he is so famous for stuttering, his case must be studied in a book like this. It is something like George Washington's fame for cutting down the cherry tree, when historians say there is not a shred of historical evidence for this incident. Or the infamous ride of a naked Lady Godiva on horseback to persuade her aristocrat husband to stop taxing peasants. Historians say there was a Lady Godiva, but no such horseback ride. Books on Washington and medieval taxation must deal with the biggest historical myths such as the cherry tree and the Lady's horseback ride.

But Demosthenes's struggle for good speech is still helpful. And for all of us, not just stutterers. Here is a boy who grew up for the most part without a father, was weak and sickly, and had a speech impediment, and who nonetheless went on by dint of perseverance and self-discipline to become one of the world's greatest orators. His story is something like that of James Earl Jones, whose voice today is legendary, and is most famous for being the voice of Darth Vader in the Star Wars movies. Jones too has a speech impediment, and nevertheless has made a career with his voice. Once again we see, as we saw with Aristotle, that impediments need not rule out significant accomplishments—even if that impediment is in one's speech.

Chapter 4

Civil War hero: Joshua Chamberlain

Joshua Chamberlain (1828–1914) was a college professor from Maine who volunteered to fight for the Union in the summer of 1862 and went on to become one of the greatest heroes of American military history. He left his wife and two children behind at the age of thirty-three because, he wrote, "there are things worth more than life and peace." "Nationality—the Law of Liberty, [and] public and private honor" were worth more to Chamberlain than his own personal safety.[23]

HELPING SAVE THE ARMY OF THE POTOMAC

Although suffering from malaria and dysentery, and commanding a vastly outnumbered regiment that had run out of ammunition, Chamberlain led a bayonet charge down Little Round Top that became one of the turning points in the Battle of Gettysburg—the July 1863 battle that turned the tide of the Civil War. His little band of unarmed men captured twice their number of armed Confederate troops, who were poised to take that hill on the farthest end of the Union line. This could have opened the way for Robert E. Lee's Army of Northern Virginia to encircle and then defeat the Northern forces. They could then have marched on the nation's capital and forced President Lincoln to recognize the Confederacy. According to an army historian, shortly after the battle,

The truth of history is, that the little brigade of Vincent's
with the self-sacrificing valor of the 20th Maine, under
the gallant leadership of Joshua L. Chamberlain, fighting
amidst the scrub-oak and rocks in that vale between the
Round Tops on the 2d of July, 1863, saved to the Union
arms the historic field of Gettysburg. Had they faltered
for one instant—had they not exceeded their actual duty
. . . there would have been no grand charge of Pickett,
and "Gettysburg" would have been the mausoleum of
departed hopes of the national cause; for [Confederate
General] Longstreet would have enveloped Little Round
Top, captured all on its crest from the rear, and held the
key of the whole position.[24]

ONE OF THE KNIGHTLIEST SOLDIERS

Chamberlain's story before and after Gettysburg is no less remarkable. He fought in nineteen other battles and many skirmishes, was
wounded six times, and had six horses shot out from under him. At
Petersburg in June 1864 (one year after Gettysburg) Chamberlain
was shot through both hips. He was left for dead by an examining
surgeon, and Maine newspapers reported that he had died. But
he recovered, and came back for more. At the end of the year, his
mother and wife pleaded with him to quit. He replied, "I am not
scared or hurt enough yet to be willing to face the rear when other
men are marching to the front." To return was the only choice
"which honor and manliness prompt."[25] His brigade participated
in a major skirmish at Quaker Road during Grant's final advance,
during which Chamberlain was wounded and nearly captured. A
major general by the end of the war, he was chosen to command
the detachment that received Lee's surrender at Appomattox. It was
his idea to order his Union soldiers to give the "carry arms" salute
to their defeated Confederate foes as a sign of respect. Recognizing
the magnanimity of that order, Confederate Major General John
B. Gordon "dropped his sword point to his boot toe in a graceful
salute to the man he would call 'one of the knightliest soldiers of
the Federal army.'"[26]

After the war Chamberlain went from glory to glory. He was elected to four successive terms as governor of Maine, the first by the largest margin in state history. After declining to run for a fifth term, he served as president of Bowdoin College for twelve years, and was a popular speaker on the lecture circuit until the end of his long life.

FIFTY YEARS OF SUFFERING

Yet this American hero carried with him two secret sources of pain—one physical and the other psychological. The first was from his wound at Petersburg. It damaged the urethra and caused urinary tract infections, severe pain, and recurring fevers for the rest of his life. The pain prevented him from walking more than one hundred feet without exhaustion, yet he continued to lead his troops into battle in the closing months of the war.[27] Surgeons installed what might have been the first-ever artificial catheter, which worked for a while. But because it was made of metal, it dropped down after a while to open up a fistula in his penis just below his scrotum. This opening never closed, so his urine was evacuated through the hole, causing him pain and embarrassment for the rest of his life. No doubt his sexual functions were impaired. Fifty years and four surgeries after Petersburg, a final infection brought on malaria, to which he succumbed at the age of eighty-five.[28] So the old warrior was finally felled by war wounds, but it took half a century.

ONE OF THE MISERIES OF LIFE

Chamberlain's other source of pain was stuttering. In a personal memoir written near the end of his life, he recalled that it was "one of the miseries" of his life. It was a "horrible stammering" that caused "sleepless anxiety" and "a serious wear upon [his] nervous system." He was naturally timid, he confessed, but the stutter added to this "bashfulness." It was "humiliating" because people "thought [him] stupid" when he could not get his words out. Worse yet, when he was a student in college a professor would "turn one gaze of contempt for which there was no synonym and write down in his rank book one of the earliest of the Arabic numerals [a low grade]." Chamberlain felt "the nerves of shame and claws of wrath curling deep within" when he could not think of a synonym for a difficult word and remained mute. But the "unkindest cut of all" was his inability to introduce mutual friends on the street or even in his room. He joked that his misfortune was that his friends' fathers "had not had their names changed by order of court" to enable Chamberlain to pronounce them.[29]

His problem, he wrote, was not being able to get out the sounds of "p," "b," and "t" when they were at the beginnings of words. Speech therapists call them "stop consonants" or "plosives." These are called "closed mutes" in many grammar books. Chamberlain added wryly that "they well nigh made one of him." His usual line of attack was to build up momentum with other words and hope that he could keep it up through these dangerous sounds. "It was at times impossible to get off a word beginning with one of these letters unless it could be launched on a wave of breath, or when, forewarned, a run could be started for it which would carry it by sheer impetus."

GLAD TO GET OUT OF TOWN

His stammering caused one of the great humiliations of his life. At the end of his senior year as a student at Bowdoin, Chamberlain was chosen, ironically, to give a speech at commencement. He had already devised a system for keeping his stuttering at bay, and we will see this system shortly. But he had not yet realized his need for a text in front of him and assiduous practice behind him.

The occasion was the fiftieth commencement of the c ollege. It was 1852 and Chamberlain was twenty-four years old. Grand dignitaries were in the audience, including the novelist Nathaniel Hawthorne and presidential candidate Franklin Pierce. Chamberlain was unnerved by the presence of "certain friends, whose love and pride were at utmost tension," and the "close-crowding and crowded galleries." His careful juggling of words and sounds suddenly collapsed; he ran out of air, opened his mouth, and not a sound emerged. "For a moment," he recalled painfully, referring to himself in the third person, "all around him swam and swayed into a mist."

> But he only reeled, half-turned, and paced the stage, grasping some evidently extemporaneous and strangely far-fetched phrases, then suddenly whirling to the front, with more blood in his face than would have flowed from Caesar's *morituri salutamus* ["We who are about to die salute you"], he delivered his conclusion straight out from the shoulder like those who are determined to die early.[30]

This is every stutterer's nightmare—sudden paralysis in front of an important audience, a catastrophe of humiliation that sabotages an occasion that could have won great glory. When it was finally over, Chamberlain confessed he was "glad to get out of town." The disgrace was too great to endure in the presence of others.

COPING AND OVERCOMING

But all was not lost. Chamberlain had already invented a method of both coping and—later—overcoming. The method was in place, and this failure would actually help the future public speaker perfect it.

The method relied on two things—self-will and "adroitness." These were two "positive measures," he observed, which were not so "taxing and wearing as the eternal round of the anxious defensive." Before he devised this system, he had lived in fear of the dreaded three consonants. Trying to speak put him through an exhausting series of losing battles as he tried vainly to ward off attacks from those enemy consonants.

At some point in college, however, the future soldier and commander resolved that "such a condition was intolerable." He would no longer try to merely avoid his enemies; instead he would go on the offensive and plan to "overcome" them.

RHYTHM AND WILL

The first tack was to realize that these closed mutes are dangerous, and so to linger about them was suicidal. Therefore "the first thing is to get away from them, as quick as possible." It "must be a touch and go. Get a good breath behind it and turn on the will." Chamberlain decided he would run from the enemy before he got captured.

But how? The solution was song. Or, in other words, rhythm. "The principle here is to summon that power of the soul which expresses itself in the sense of rhythm." When he would sense that he was coming to a difficult sound, he would sing. "Catch the pulse of time," he told himself. "Feel the emotion of it, and that will bear you on its motion."

The key was to give himself up to what he called "the trance." This was easier, apparently, if "the occasion [was] a great one." He would try to give himself "freely to the rhythmic sway and swing." He recalled that the Spartans used to sing their laws for after-dinner entertainment ("and the Spartan laws were no laughing matter"). He would not be "ashamed" if some laughed or thought it odd, but at the same time he tried to be "circumspect" and avoid undue "awkwardness."

Chamberlain testified that this method worked "nine times out of ten." He learned from his first commencement speech to practice and practice, and not to try to speak from memory. Three years later (1855) Chamberlain gave another commencement address after earning his master's degree at Bowdoin, and it went off without a hitch.[31] Chamberlain no doubt continued to practice his method as he taught day in and day out for six years as a college professor until he left for war in 1862. The practice continued, and his skills at skipping lightly over his enemy consonants were further honed in his years as governor, college president, and speaker on the lecture circuit.

If Chamberlain did not reduce this enemy to unconditional surrender, he kept it on the defensive. The stutter was never completely defeated, for he wrote near the end of his life that its effects reached "the whole of life." But he declared victory nonetheless: his stratagems to trick the stutter demon proved that seemingly intractable obstacles "can be surmounted."[32]

HOW STUTTERING HELPED CHAMBERLAIN

Before concluding this chapter, it might be worth considering how stuttering might have helped Chamberlain. In other words, we should ask whether Chamberlain accomplished more than just "surmounting" this obstacle which he called "horrible." The answer is that yes, the character which was formed in this early battle with his tongue seems to have contributed to forming the remarkable soldier and leader he grew to become.

It started with self-discipline. The steely eyed determination that inspired men on the battlefield was forged as a young man battling books, languages, and a stammer. When he was nineteen he secluded himself in his family's attic from 5:00 AM to 10:00 PM every day to study rhetoric, classics, theology, and foreign languages so that he could pass entrance exams to Bowdoin College. Once admitted, he used that same rigor to attack classical Greek, memorizing a whole grammar book "from alphabet to appendix."[33] By the time he went off to war Chamberlain had learned eleven languages. It was this mental discipline that Chamberlain used to fight stuttering. Just as he had refused to let other intellectual obstacles stop him, he resolved at some point during college that he would no longer put up with "sleepless anxiety" and humiliation.

The result was the two-pronged attack we saw earlier, using the will for firepower and rhythm for maneuvering. The attack was repeated from then on, succeeding nine times out of ten. These victories no doubt reminded him on the battlefield that determination and canniness could overcome great obstacles. So his stuttering seems to have become an asset at war. By showing him how an iron will and creative imagination could subdue a powerful foe, it gave him the confidence that these same weapons could succeed against new enemies.

Self-discipline and strength of will—strengthened by innumerable battles with the stuttering demon—were also key to Chamberlain's legendary courage. These qualities enabled him to march eighty miles in four days in a blistering sun on the way to Gettysburg, while suffering from malaria and sun stroke—not to mention enduring three days of battle after getting there.[34] It took courage and determination to launch a bayonet drive from the top of Little Round Top on the second day of battle after his officers shouted to him they were "annihilated" because they were out of ammunition.[35] In battle after battle following Gettysburg, Chamberlain repeatedly led troops into battle despite pain and danger; his men marveled at his coolness under fire.

IF ANYONE WANTS TO KILL ME, HERE I AM!

After the War, Chamberlain's courage was displayed again. In 1879 Maine was in the midst of a constitutional crisis that was reported day by day in newspapers across the nation. The Democratic Party had used trickery to get their candidates into the legislature, Republicans were enraged, and a United States (Republican) Senator from Maine called for a popular uprising.

Chamberlain was the head of the state militia, the governor had ended his term, and the legislature was not in session. Republicans urged Chamberlain to call out the militia, and Democrats declared that he must enforce law and order by taking their side. Chamberlain refused to take either side, and decided that calling out the militia would provoke a riot. He insisted that everyone wait for the Maine Supreme Court to decide the matter. He was offered bribes by both sides, and received death threats. When an aide rushed into his office in the statehouse to warn that a crowd of thirty men bent on killing him was forming outside, Chamberlain hurried out and faced the mob.

Men, you wished to kill me, I hear. Killing is no new thing
to me. I have offered myself to be killed many times,
when I no more deserved it than I do now. Some of you,
I think, have been with me in those days. You understand
what you want, do you? I am here to preserve the peace
and honor of this State, until the rightful government is
seated—whichever it may be, it is not for me to say. But it
is for me to see that the laws of this state are put into effect, without fraud, without force, but with calm thought
and sincere purpose. I am here for that, and I shall do it.
If anyone wants to kill me for it, here I am. Let him kill![36]

Alice Trulock reports that Chamberlain threw back his coat and
looked at the men straight in the eye. In the startled silence an
old veteran pushed his way forward and shouted, "By God, old
General, the first man that dares to lay a hand on you, I'll kill him
on the spot!" The mob slowly dispersed.[37]

COURAGE, HUMOR, AND STUTTERING

Courage enabled Chamberlain to display humor in the midst of
pain. When he was struck by the bullet at Petersburg that shot
through both hips, his first reaction (according to an interview
in 1904) was humor: "The first pain I felt was in my back and I
thought, What will my mother say—her boy shot in the back?
Then I saw the blood gushing from my side and I felt better."[38]

Of course Chamberlain's courage, intelligence, and cleverness
were not formed by his battles with stuttering alone. There was
also his Calvinist trust in divine sovereignty, which helped keep
him calm in danger and professional frustration. After recovering
from his injury at Petersburg he explained in a letter to his parents
that he felt confident to return to battle because "I can trust my
own life & the welfare of my family in the hands of Providence."[39]
When he still had not been promoted six months after Gettysburg,
Chamberlain wrote his wife Fannie, "Everything will be all right,
I know. Men may not do right towards me, but Providence will."[40]

Not that Providence necessarily approved of everything in Chamberlain's life. He was not perfect. His accounts of his battles were not always the most accurate, he might have subordinated his wife to his professional ambitions, and he exhibited less than exemplary attitudes toward African Americans and Catholics that were typical of Protestants of that era. And, according to one historian, after the war Chamberlain was "too willing to use his name and reputation to lure investors into business ventures in which he himself did not invest."[41]

Like any figure in history, Chamberlain was a complex character. His stuttering was only a part of the mystery of the man. Nevertheless, the evidence suggests that the persistence and inventiveness which he used to assault the stuttering demon helped shape his character. Without that character he might never have become the war hero and honorable statesman this nation has come to revere. Chamberlain said as much when toward the end of his life he wrote his "Early Memoir." There he observed that his struggle for oral mastery "affected habits and perhaps character, and the indirect effects . . . may have reached into the whole of life." Through this agony of soul and tongue he came to know "that obstacles irremovable can be surmounted."[42] In other words, the confidence he gained from surmounting the irremovable obstacle of stuttering helped Chamberlain surmount later obstacles in both war and peace.

Chapter 5

The king who gave "The Speech":
George VI

In 1938 *Time* magazine called King George VI (1895–1952) "the most famed contemporary stammerer" in the world.[43] He was the monarch of the British Empire, which at that time included almost one third of humanity. Much of the world knew that this very famous and powerful man was struggling with a disability that paralyzes millions of its afflicted. The recent movie *The King's Speech* (2010) has brought that struggle to life.

The movie won many awards, including Best Picture, Best Director, and Best Actor at the Academy Awards. But like almost all movies, it took dramatic license with the real story. For example, it portrayed a conflict between the king and his Australian speech therapist that did not exist. The king, as far as we know, never insulted his therapist. But more importantly, it suggested that the king was never able to master his unruly tongue until he was coached by his therapist just before his coronation in May, 1937. In reality, he had been coached by that same therapist, Lionel Logue, for more than a decade by that time, and had reached a breakthrough in 1926. In any event, the movie highlighted what was a fascinating and important life in our modern history.

A DIFFICULT CHILDHOOD

As a young prince, Albert—or "Bertie," as the future king was called by his family—had a hard go of it. His mother was cold and undemonstrative—both physically and emotionally—toward Bertie and his brother Edward, and her husband King George V was critical and controlling toward his children. Bertie was afraid of his father, and his father intended him to be so. "I was always frightened of my father," George V told a confidant, "[and] they must be frightened of me."[44] He set high standards for his children, and did not seem to care that some of these expectations put his children into terrifying situations. For example, George V and Queen Mary made the children memorize and recite poetry before invited guests, even when it was clear that one of their sons could not perform without considerable delay and anguish. When Bertie stammered and halted, unable to pronounce a word, his father would bark, "Get it out!"

It wasn't only poetry, of course. At seven he could not say "fraction" in math class at school because of the initial "f." This caused him to go silent when called on, which only made his teachers think he was stupid or stubborn. At eight the sounds "k" and "kw" were impossible, so he could never say "king" or "queen."

Even though the young prince was always athletic, and turned out to have terrific eye-hand coordination (later in life he was an excellent skeet shooter), he was also small. And because of his stuttering, he was shy. As a result, he was teased and bullied, even by his own brothers and sister. When he was a thirteen-year-old student at the Royal Naval College, he was left tied up in a hammock until his cries for help eventually brought release.

A YOUNG MAN'S AGONIES

In some ways, things got worse as the prince became a young man. Now he was expected to represent the Crown by giving speeches. So when he was eighteen on the final six-month training cruise to qualify him as a midshipman and regular member of the Royal

Navy, the cruiser *Cumberland* stopped at Jamaica in the West In-
dies, and Prince Albert was asked to make a speech to open the
Kingston Yacht Club. Poor Albert stuttered his way through a prepared speech while local schoolgirls vied to see who could touch
his trousers the most while he was standing on a platform above
them.

Two years later Albert's navigating officer on another ship
told of how he had just met the "small, red-faced youth with a stutter. . . . When he [brought his picket boat alongside my ship] he
gave a sort of stutter and an explosion [of sound from his mouth]. I
had no idea who he was and very nearly cursed him for spluttering
at me!"[45]

Three years later, when he was twenty-two, he had another of
a long series of gastric illnesses, and had to leave the battleship *Ma-
laya* for a hospital. Recurring stomach troubles and ulcers, perhaps
caused by anxiety over his stammering, on top of the daily mental
torture of being unable to speak fluently, threw him into despair.
He concluded that he would have to give up his naval career, despite having spent eight years training and serving on ships. He felt
like a failure.

The prince's marriage in 1923 to Elizabeth was welcome re-
spite. She was compassionate and devoted, his best friend and loyal
ally. Most important, she was the source of encouragement and
consolation that he needed in times of frustration.

But the frustration continued nonetheless. Robert Hyde reported that when Prince Albert was leaving a group of workers
or boys at a summer camp, "he would feel that he was expected
to wave his hand and wish them 'good-bye' or, as [his brother] the
Prince of Wales would have done, the less formal 'Cheerio.' But at
the last moment he would be overcome with diffidence and for
the next ten minutes feel miserable and angry with himself for his
omission."[46] He hesitated waving because it would require a short
verbal greeting that he was afraid he could not utter. But then he
would regret not doing so, and wonder if he could have uttered the
words after all. The self-doubts and self-recriminations were endless. Sometimes the frustrations threw the prince into fits of rage.

The humiliations continued. Once when addressing a group of farmers from an open-air cart, he could say nothing but a "painful, wordless mumble for several minutes."[47] When his wife accompanied him to public events, her knuckles would turn white during his speeches as she gripped the edge of a table in anxiety for her husband.

The prince seemed to hit bottom at the age of thirty. It was 1925 and the opening of the British Empire Exhibition at Wembley Stadium. One hundred thousand people came out to see the festivities and hear the future king. Millions more were tuned to their radios all over the empire, waiting expectantly for the prince to speak. But Albert was tongue-tied. There were long, unnatural pauses, agonizing silences as he moved his jaw muscles frantically, but without producing a sound.

After this debacle, the prince despaired. He had had speech therapists in the previous years, but to no avail. He feared there might be something wrong with him mentally. This was one of the dominant theories in the very young field of speech therapy—that stuttering was rooted in the emotions, and so stutterers had deep emotional problems, perhaps mental illness. Maybe, he and many others feared, he was unfit for public life.

Bertie didn't know it, but in the vast audience that day at Wembley was a forty-five-year-old Australian speech therapist. After listening to the prince's tortured attempts to speak, Lionel Logue leaned over to his son and said, "He's too old for me to manage a complete cure. But I could very nearly do it. I'm sure of it."[48]

BREAKTHROUGH

Of Irish descent, Logue had perfected his speech therapy by helping shell-shocked Australian soldiers coming home from gas attacks in France in World War I. Some had gone from being mute to normal speaking under Logue's tutelage. When Buckingham Palace asked Eileen Macleod, founding member of the Society of Speech Therapists, for a therapist for the prince, Macleod recommended Logue. She had two reasons. She thought the prince's stuttering was caused by his father the king's impatience, and that another man—kinder and gentler—might be able to undo the emotional damage wreaked by George V. Second, he was an Aussie, and so would not be overawed by a prince.

Macleod was convinced that the relationship needed to be as much as possible between equals. Elizabeth, Albert's wife, accepted Macleod's recommendation because the couple was scheduled to make a trip to New Zealand and Australia, and the prince would have to make a round of speeches in both those lands.

Logue later remarked that when the prince came to his office for his first appointment, his eyes looked tired and hopeless. But by the end of the first visit, which lasted two hours, "you could see that there was hope once more in his heart."[49]

What suddenly gave hope after years of failed therapies? Logue told the prince that stutterers are not freaks but ordinary people with a disability. And that the disability was not mental or emotional but physical. The prince had been breathing and using his muscles incorrectly for a whole lifetime, and the bad habits needed to be replaced with good habits—breathing properly and relaxing the muscles of the speech apparatus. It would take great effort and self-discipline. But if the prince was willing to work hard—very hard—he had every chance of near-complete recovery.

Prince Albert was thrilled. The problem was not some kind of mental illness after all but something in the way he was moving his lungs and diaphragm and muscles around the jaw. If he would practice moving all these body parts in the right way, he could learn how to talk all over again. And . . . speak with some degree of fluency.

Logue instructed the prince to stand in front of a window and practice his breathing—slowly and carefully. He was to stand there for one hour each day intoning all his vowels for fifteen seconds each. He was to practice breathing from his diaphragm and stop breathing with shallow breaths from his upper chest. He was to speak slowly and deliberately, and not try to blurt out words quickly.

The prince started noticing improvement almost immediately. After a few months, and just before he and the duchess were scheduled to sail to the land down under, the prince decided to make a dry run. It was bold, because it was a meeting of the Pilgrims' Society, a dining club filled with some of England's most gifted speakers, hosted by the former prime minister and noted orator Lord Balfour. To everyone's delight that night, the Prince was "a smiling, confident speaker who, although no great orator, spoke with a surprising confidence and conviction."[50]

In New Zealand Albert gave three speeches the first morning he was there. He wrote his mother Queen Mary, "The last one in the Town Hall [was] quite a long one, & I can tell you that I was really pleased with the way I made it, as I had perfect confidence in myself & I did not hesitate at all. Logue's teaching is still working well, but of course if I get tired it still worries me."[51]

When he got to Australia in April (1927), the prince wrote to Logue. "I have ever so much more confidence in myself and don't brood over a speech as in the old days. I know what to do now, and the knowledge has helped me over and over again."[52] Days later in Canberra he made a speech in the open air to 20,000 people, to open the door of the new Parliament House with a golden key. It went off, he wrote his father, "without a hitch, & I did not hesitate once."[53]

British newspapers took notice after the duke and duchess returned to England. Reporting in June 1928 on a speech at a fundraising banquet for a children's hospital in London, the *Standard* noted, "The Duke has vastly improved as a speaker and his hesitation has almost entirely gone." In October that year the *Evening News* observed, "The Duke of York grows in fluency as a speaker. He is markedly more confident than he was two years ago, more confident, indeed, than he was a few months ago."[54] Even the *Pittsburgh Press* got wind of the duke's recovery. Its December 1, 1928 front page proclaimed, "The Duke of York is the happiest man in the British Empire. He no longer stutters." The story told of the duke's speech defect, Logue's work with him over the previous two years, and the remarkable transformation that had occurred. The newspaper related how the duchess had previously done the talking for her husband. But now, "she hangs back, shyly watching the man of whom she is obviously proud."[55]

THE KING'S SPEECHES

The prince enjoyed almost a decade of peace and success before a new crisis arose. His father, King George V, died in January, 1936, and was succeeded by Albert's brother David, who assumed the title of Edward VIII. But in December of that year the new king announced that he was abdicating the throne because of his love for Wallis Simpson, an American divorcee. When Albert heard the news several weeks before the public announcement, he was filled with "an agony of apprehension."[56] He dreaded the prospect of becoming king, with the endless speeches the office would entail. Of course he had enjoyed general success by using Logue's techniques, but he still had his fears. Occasionally he still struggled with words starting with "c" and "g," and words with a double "s" such as "oppression" and "suppression" were sometimes difficult. What if the muscle spasms in his jaw and cheeks returned, such as they still did from time to time?

The nervous tension finally exploded when it became certain that he would ascend the throne. The government and family had considered skipping Albert and crowning his younger brother the Duke of Kent, but decided against it because of his history of drug abuse. When Albert was named as the new heir, he found solace with his mother. "I broke down," he told his diary, "& sobbed like a child."[57]

The new king's fears seemed confirmed when in a practice session two days before his May 1937 coronation, he stuttered on his spoken parts in the ceremony. This made him "almost hysterical," but his wife, the new queen, calmed him down.[58]

The coronation went beautifully. King George VI spoke well after all. The millions listening both in England and abroad were surprised by how fluent he sounded. He gave a coronation address at the end of that long day. *Time* said his voice was "warm and strong."[59] The *Detroit Free Press* wrote with astonishment that "many persons are classifying him with President Roosevelt as possessing a perfect radio voice."[60]

Logue was exhausted after putting in long days and nights preparing the king for the ceremony. But for the king, it was a triumph that gave him new confidence. Gradually his pauses became shorter and the rhythm in his slow and steady speaking became less monotonous. A speech to Parliament that fall was a big success. The *Sunday Express* noted that "he spoke slowly but there was no hesitation or stammer. Indeed, the words took on a dignity and actual beauty from the tempo that he had wisely imposed on himself."[61]

The speeches continued to go well for another two years. Then Nazi Germany invaded Poland on September 1, 1939. World War II had begun, and just weeks later George VI became the commander in chief of a nation at war.

WAR LEADER

Winston Churchill, England's prime minister during the war, had high praise for King George VI as a war king. Churchill said, "I made certain he was kept informed of every secret matter; and the care and thoroughness with which he mastered the immense daily flow of State papers made a deep mark on my mind."[62] The young king knew that his position gave him no official power in the conduct of the war, but he also knew that it was "his duty to advise, to counsel, and to warn[,] and the use which he made of this duty, together with the closeness and mutual respect between him and his wartime Prime Minister, meant that his influence was more than merely symbolic."[63]

His wartime speeches in particular were far more than symbolic. In May 1940, for example, the king gave a speech to the nation just after France had fallen to the Nazis and British troops were stranded at Dunkirk, threatened with obliteration. After several days of preparation, the king told Britain and a world listening in, "The decisive struggle is now upon us. . . . it is no mere territorial conquest that our enemies are seeking. It is the overthrow, complete and final, of this Empire and of everything for which it stands, and after that the conquest of the world."[64]

The speech was an instant success. Morale went up all over the country and beyond. The king said "it was easily my best effort."[65]

When the Blitz started in September of that year, with German bombers eventually taking 43,000 civilian lives before it ended in May 1941, the king and his queen became favorites of the masses. They refused to leave London, even though a million homes in the city alone were damaged and destroyed, and Buckingham Palace itself was hit. The royal couple spent at least a third of every day touring areas hit by bombs, talking to thousands who had lost loved ones and whose homes were shattered. The king became known as a royal who could talk unpretentiously and directly to people—a king who cared. *Time* crowed, "Never in British history has a monarch seen and talked to so many of his subjects or so fully shared their life."[66]

Perhaps these months of talking to ordinary people in their suffering gave the king a new sense of authority. His Christmas speech of 1941 is considered among his finest. He told the British world that the message of Christmas was one "of thankfulness and hope—of thankfulness to the Almighty for his great mercies, of hope for the return to this earth of peace and good will." He spoke of the great contributions made by other nations in the British Empire, and more recently by the Americans. He ended by telling a story once told by Abraham Lincoln about a boy carrying a smaller boy up a hill. "Isn't that a heavy burden?," the older boy was asked. The response was, "It's not a burden, it's my brother."[67]

At this point in the war, the British were relieved that the United States had finally entered the war just weeks earlier, after the attack on Pearl Harbor on December 7. The story about burdens and brothers was an implicit tribute to this new alliance, long informal and now formal. The king and queen had visited America in 1939, when FDR and George VI started what became a close friendship. This relationship helped cement the critical wartime alliance between the two nations. The king's official biographer observed that the shared experience of struggling with a disability—the president's polio and the king's stuttering—helped bond these two men together.[68]

We don't know if Roosevelt heard the king's Christmas speech, but the press was impressed. According to the *Glasgow Herald*, "Both in manner and in matter, The King's broadcast yesterday was the most mature and inspiriting that he has yet made."

The king himself was pleased. On the day after the speech, he wrote Logue a handwritten letter.

> My dear Logue,
>
> I'm so glad that my broadcast went off so well yesterday. I felt altogether different and I had no fear of the microphone. I am sure that those visits that you have paid me [there were eighty-two sessions by the end of his life] have done me a great deal of good and I must keep them up during the new year.
> Thank you so very much for all your help.
> With all good wishes for 194[2]
> I am
>
> Yours very sincerely
>
> George R.I.[69]

The king grew so confident in his ability to be fluent that he sent Logue home to have dinner with his family while the king delivered his annual Christmas speech in 1944. Just a few weeks earlier, in a speech marking the disbanding of the Home Guard, he even stuttered deliberately on one word so that "people might . . . know it was me."[70]

But the war took its toll on the king, and on his speech. When he gave a speech in May 1945 to mark the end of the war in Europe, he was burned out—and it showed. He was tired, and hesitated far more than usual. One listener wrote that his words were excellent, "but it is agony to listen to him—like a typewriter that sticks at every third word." The film of the broadcast shown a week later showed a face that appeared "wizened and lined," his mouth twitching with efforts to control his stutter.[71]

There was not much relief after the war, as the king presided over enormous changes coming to Britain—the beginning of the welfare state, the end of Britain's go-it-alone foreign policy, nationalization of much of British industry, and the postwar decline in deference.[72]

The exhaustion of conscientious leadership, compounded by chain smoking for much of his adult life, led to a premature death from lung cancer at age fifty-seven in 1952. His subjects mourned.

STUTTERING AND CHARACTER

King George VI has gone down in history as a people's monarch known for his sense of duty and decency. He gained a reputation for integrity and courage—the latter of which was vividly displayed not only during the Battle of Britain but also in his lifelong battle with his tongue. It might even be said that his character was shaped in part by that battle with his tongue, for it was the agony of stuttering that helped develop qualities in him that proved to be endearing to millions.

For example, he was said to be the most humane in his family, especially in his feeling for the suffering of Britons during the war. Who can doubt that his own suffering feelings of humiliation and inferiority for much of his life helped him empathize with the sufferings of his countrymen?

King George was said to be a much better listener than his father. One can be certain that hesitancy to speak will make any person a better listener. The thousands whom he comforted by his presence and listening ear might never have guessed that it was this disability that helped make their king such a beloved one.

George VI was also well-known for his hard work and dogged determination. Lionel Logue said this was the secret to his near-conquest of stuttering. "No man ever worked as hard as he did," the Aussie therapist wrote, "and achieved such a grand result."[73]

But there was another factor—one that might explain why many other therapists were completely unsuccessful with the royal stutterer, and only Logue could coach him to fluency. The answer to this riddle lies in the words of Logue's daughter-in-law Anne, who became a consultant in child psychiatry at a teaching hospital in Middlesex, England: "[My father-in-law] was a super good daddy where George V had been a ghastly one."[74] In other words, Logue gave the prince-then-king the patience and faith which he never got from his own father. In a word, he gave him love.

Chapter 6

The strange roar of "The Last Lion": Churchill

One of Winston Churchill's earliest speeches in Parliament was a disaster. It was 1904, when Churchill (1874–1965) was thirty years old. He had been elected to Parliament four years earlier on the strength of his war exploits and oratorical powers. But in the midst of a speech championing the cause of labor unions, he broke down.

Until this point he had memorized all his speeches, standing up without notes. But on this spring evening, while in the midst of urging support for the labor classes, his mind went blank. He repeated the last phrase that had come out of his mouth, hoping that would trigger his memory, but to no avail. He sank down in his seat and buried his face in his hands.

From that point on to the end of his career, Churchill prepared doggedly for his speeches, taking six to eight hours to prepare a forty-minute speech. He never again stood up to deliver a major address without putting notes in front of himself. In fact, he had his secretaries type out his speeches double-spaced, in rhythmic psalm-like fashion, and added his own notes on where to stress words or speak slowly. William Manchester says Churchill "practice[ed] endlessly in front of mirrors" to get the wording and sounds right. He also tried to anticipate criticisms, so part of the practice was "fashioning ripostes to this or that party."[75]

STRANGE MIXTURE

One reason for the long hours of preparation and practice seems to have been a strange mixture of speech impediments. Churchill had always conceded that while writing the English language came naturally, he had to work hard to become an effective speaker. We all know that he became one of the most forceful orators of the twentieth century—despite never attending university and being rated the stupidest boy in his boarding school.[76] But by his own admission and that of those who knew him, it was by indefatigable practice that he compensated for his speech defects and became a brilliant speaker anyway.

There was at least one reason for his practice that all agree on—he had a lisp that seems to have been caused by a birth defect. His son Randolph writes, "All his life Churchill suffered from an impediment in his speech. It is hard to define exactly what it was; some thought it was a stammer: some a lisp. Certainly, like his father before him, he always had a difficulty in pronouncing the letter 's' . . . . We also have the evidence of Mrs. Muriel Warde, formerly Muriel Wilson, who has told the author [Randolph Churchill] of how when she was a young girl at Tranby Croft, Churchill used to walk up and down the long drive rehearsing such phrases as, 'The Spanish ships I cannot see for they are not in sight.' This was designed to cure him of his trouble in pronouncing the sibilant 's.'"[77]

TONGUE-TIED

According to Dr. John Mather, writing for the Churchill Centre and Museum in London, before he returned to India in 1897 Churchill was told by an American masseuse that his tongue was "restrained by a ligament which nobody else has." This, he thought, provided "the true explanation of my speaking through my nose." When he asked a throat specialist about cutting the ligament, the doctor refused to do so. Mather says Churchill then told his mother that he was still tongue "tied."[78] According to some biographers, all that Churchill meant by this was that he lisped.

But as Churchill's own son suggested ("some thought it was a stammer"), it was not so simple as that. After Churchill escaped from a prisoner-of-war camp in the Transvaal of South Africa, the Boers put out a description of their prisoner on the loose: He was "about 5 ft 8 or 9 inches, blonde with light thin small moustache, walks with slight stoop, cannot speak any Dutch, during long conversations he occasionally makes a rattling noise in his throat."[79] A lisp does not sound like rattling.

Manchester's description adds to the complexity: "Because of his lisp, *and* because he growled so often, his speech was often hard to follow."[80] When he writes of Churchill as a late teen at boarding school, Manchester adds that "except for his *stammer*, a speech impediment which was just becoming evident, and a certain guttural quality which was developing in his reedy adolescent voice," Churchill's attempts to speak before a mirror went well.[81]

SINGING IN THE BATHTUB

There is more circumstantial evidence. Churchill often conceived of and developed his speeches in the bathtub. He also practiced them there. Manchester tells us that one of his principal methods of practice was to sing them, "not in the virile baritone familiar in Parliament, but in a soft, high tone."[82] Those who lisp know that singing does not help one to articulate an "s" properly. But stutterers know that singing enables almost all stutterers to get through difficult sounds. They also know that it loosens up the vocal chords, reducing the chance that they will suddenly block on a sound.

There is also an abundance of direct testimony from those who knew him or studied his life. Louis Adamic wrote in 1946 of a conversation he had over dinner with Roosevelt and Churchill at the White House:

> "Someone sent me a . . . c-corn-cob pipe," said Churchill and stuck his fat cigar into his mouth, making it glow.
>
> "I received one too," FDR said. "I get several a year."

"Is yours . . . w-worm-eaten too?" asked Churchill.

Adamic adds that when he introduced himself to Churchill, the British prime minister replied, "I am r-reading your book, and I-I find it—int'r-resting."[83]

"WHEN HE GETS EXCITED"

After traveling with Churchill throughout America on a lecture tour in 1931, Louis Alber wrote, "Winston Churchill grew up with a lisp and a stutter, the result of a defect in his palate. It is characteristic of the man's perseverance that, despite this handicap, he has made himself one of the greatest orators of all time. Churchill has never cured the lisp. And the stutter still breaks out when he gets excited—which is often."[84]

A writer for Australia's 1937 issue of *Current Notes on International Affairs* wrote of one of Churchill's speeches, "Mr. Churchill was at times difficult to follow, his stammer being very apparent."[85]

New York Supreme Court justice James W. Gerard recalled in the late 1940s that when he first met Churchill, the future prime minister was "without the forcefulness that he possesses today, and he suffered at times from a slight stutter."[86]

Churchill's personal physician recorded in his diary that his patient "grew up full of apprehension and he spoke with a stutter."[87] Konrad Adenauer, the first chancellor of West Germany after WWII, observed that Churchill's speech in his later years was "jerky, sometimes stuttering, hesitating, indecisive, until suddenly four, five sentences emerge which are reminiscent of the big stones of an enormous building."[88]

So there you have it. Churchill labored all his life against a complex combination of speech defects that included a lisp and a stutter.

TRICK OF ORATORY?

But what I just wrote is controversial. The popular historian Paul Johnson asserts that Churchill "had no disabilities other than a slight lisp," and Dr. John Mather insists that it is a "myth" that Churchill was a stutterer.[89] Since Mather's article is on the website of the International Churchill Society, this demurral must be taken seriously.[90]

Mather cites Churchill's own statement that a doctor declared in 1897 that he had no physical defect related to his speech. Yet at the same time Mather relates the story—without discounting it—of the masseuse declaring that Churchill had a strange ligament hindering his speech. Mather also testifies that a doctor refused to snip it, and that Churchill himself told his mother that he was tongue-tied. By Mather's own admission, there seems to have been something wrong physically after all.

Mather then protests that Churchill's family never mentioned a stutter. Yet we have already seen that Churchill's son Randolph concedes that some think his father had a stammer. Mather discounts one secretary's story (that he stuttered when he got excited) by claiming none of the others mentioned it to others or him. Why would she make this up? Perhaps the others did not think it worth mentioning if the lisp was more noticeable.

Mather attributes the impression of stuttering to Churchill's "trick of oratory." It was merely his groping for words, according to Mather, sometimes inadvertent and sometimes purposeful as a "loaded pause" for rhetorical effect.

Perhaps this was the case in his speeches where he was more fully in control. Many stutterers have an easier time giving a speech than in everyday conversation where the give and take robs the stutterer of control. This would explain why Churchill's contemporaries said that he tended to stutter when in conversation and when he got excited.

Perhaps Mather and the Churchill Society dismiss reports of a stutter because there are so few signs of it in his recorded speeches. But this may simply be the result of Churchill's relentless determination to practice and master his oratory. There is no doubt that he had a lisp and something else that was odd in his speech. There is also no doubt that he compensated for these with a nearly scientific approach to the speech-making process.

UNFORGETTABLE HUMOR

Thankfully, this combination of speech problems did not keep Churchill's mouth closed. He used his tongue with preternatural effect. Some of the most memorable utterances have been unforgettably funny. For example, when Lady Astor at a dinner told him, "Winston, if I were your wife I'd poison your soup," Churchill replied, "Nancy, if I were your husband I'd drink it." After he had crossed swords with John Foster Dulles, Churchill called him "the only bull who brings his own china shop with him," and coined the progression, "dull, duller, Dulles."[91]

Churchill maintained a long rivalry with Clement Atlee, the Labour Party leader who defeated Churchill in the 1945 election to become prime minister. When Atlee went to Moscow and left his fellow Labour politicians behind, Churchill quipped, "When the mouse is gone, the cats will play." Churchill called Atlee "a sheep in sheep's clothing" and "a modest man with much to be modest about."[92]

When a young MP had delivered an emotional appeal for unilateral disarmament and asked Churchill after what he thought, the latter replied, "Why, I thought it was very good. It must have been good, for it contained, so far as I know, all the platitudes known to the human race, with the possible exceptions of 'Prepare to meet thy God' and 'Please adjust your dress before leaving.'"[93]

On Churchill's seventy-fifth birthday a photographer said, "I hope, sir, that I will shoot your picture on your hundredth birthday." The old man replied, "I don't see why not, young man. You look reasonably fit and healthy."[94]

LEGENDARY ORATOR

Nor did his speech problems keep Churchill from becoming one of the last century's most legendary orators. His eloquence was natural and exalted. According to one contemporary writing about his speeches, "There was nothing false, inflated, artificial in his eloquence. It was his natural idiom. His world was built and fashioned in heroic lines. He spoke its language."[95] And his informal oratory over (usually) long dinners, while unpracticed, was no less impressive. Harold MacMillan, a later British prime minister, recalled the dinner meetings with Churchill, who was then chancellor of the Exchequer, and young Conservative backbenchers in the late 1920s:

> All the rest of us would sit around, sometimes late into the night, smoking, drinking, and arguing and of course listening. The flow of Churchill's rhetoric once it got under way was irresistible. Nevertheless, he quite naturally allowed rival themes to be put forward.[96]

One of his best-remembered speeches was the one he gave before Parliament on June 4, 1940, as France was collapsing before the Nazi juggernaut. It provides a taste of the way his combination of bluntness and gracefulness could be inspiring.

> Even though large tracts of Europe and many old and famous States have fallen or may fall into the grip of the Gestapo and all the odious apparatus of Nazi rule, we shall not flag or fail. We shall go on to the end. We shall fight in France, we shall fight on the seas and oceans, we shall fight with growing confidence and growing strength in the air. We shall defend our Island, whatever the cost may be. We shall fight on the beaches, we shall fight on the landing grounds, we shall fight in the fields and in the streets, we shall fight in the hills. We shall never surrender, and even if, which I do not for a moment believe, this island or a large part of it were subjugated and starving, then our Empire beyond the seas, armed and guarded by the British Fleet, would carry on the struggle, until, in

God's good time, the new world, with all its power and
might, steps forth to the liberation of the old.[97]

Several opposition party (Labour) members wept, and one Labour
leader wrote, "That was worth 1000 [guns] & [was] the speech of
1000 years."[98]

Just two weeks later Churchill rallied the nation again. In a
speech which the *New York Times* has recently called "one of the
greatest ever delivered by an Englishman" because of its soaring
oratory—and because it is believed to have sealed the British
determination to fight Hitler after the fall of France—Churchill
called his countrymen to "their finest hour."

> What General Weygand called the Battle of France is
> over. I expect that the Battle of Britain is about to be-
> gin. Upon this battle depends the survival of Christian
> civilization. Upon it depends our own British life, and
> the long continuity of our institutions and our Empire.
> The whole fury and might of the enemy must very soon
> be turned on us. Hitler knows that he will have to break
> us in this island or lose the war. If we can stand up to
> him, all Europe may be free and the life of the world may
> move forward into broad, sunlit uplands. But if we fail,
> then the whole world, including the United States, in-
> cluding all that we have known and cared for, will sink
> into the abyss of a new Dark Age made more sinister,
> and perhaps more protracted, by the lights of perverted
> science. Let us therefore brace ourselves to our duties
> and so bear ourselves that, if the British Empire and its
> Commonwealth last for a thousand years, men will still
> say, "This was their finest hour."[99]

SELF-CONFIDENCE

How can we account for such prodigious orations coming from a
man who struggled all his life with handicaps of speech? Part of it
was his self-confidence. Violet Bonham Carter, daughter of H. H.
Asquith, a later prime minister, remembers a dinner party in 1906

when Churchill, struck by her beauty, asked her age (he had not yet married). She replied that she was nineteen.

> "And I," he said almost despairingly, "am thirty-two already. Younger than anyone else who *counts*, though," he added, as if to comfort himself. Then savagely: "Curse ruthless time! Curse our mortality. How cruelly short is the allotted span for all we must cram into it!" And he burst forth into an eloquent diatribe on the shortness of human life, the immensity of possible human accomplishment—a theme so well exploited by the poets, prophets and philosophers of all ages that it might seem difficult to invest it with a new and startling significance. Yet for me he did so, in a torrent of magnificent language which appeared to be both effortless and inexhaustible and ended up with the words I shall always remember: "We are all worms. But I do believe that I am a *glow*worm."[100]

UNRELENTING EFFORT

He might have been a glowworm, but he also displayed the unrelenting effort of the inchworm. According to Manchester, he had once said that throughout his youth "it was my only ambition to be master of the spoken word."[101] We have already seen that he practiced hours and hours before a speech. When he was congratulated for a short speech to a small group that was thought to be improvised, he snapped, "Improvised be damned! I thought of it this morning in my bath and I wish now I hadn't wasted it on this little crowd."[102] He would dictate a speech's first draft to a secretary, often while pacing around a room, then revise and revise, add asides and little notes to the final draft, and finally practice reciting out loud, often singing in a high voice.

Of course Churchill was in a class by himself. Most of us would despair after trying to match even a few of his enormous gifts. His genius was already noticed by an upperclassman at his boarding school.

> I was greatly attracted by this extraordinary boy. His commanding intelligence, his bravery, charm, and indifference to ugly surroundings, vivid imagination. Descriptive powers, general knowledge of the world and of history—gained no one knew how, but never disputed—and above all that magnetism and sympathy which shone in his eyes, and radiated from a personality which—even under the severe repression of our public school system—dominated great numbers around him, many of whom were his superiors in age and prowess.[103]

As Manchester has observed, Churchill's gifts were so many that it is impossible to sum the man up: "He was too many people. If ever there was a Renaissance man, he was it. In the age of the specialist, he was the antithesis, our Leonardo. As a writer, he was a reporter, novelist, essayist, critic, historian, and biographer. As a statesman he served, before becoming His Majesty's first magistrate, as minister for the colonies and for trade, home affairs, finance, and all three of the armed forces. Away from his desk he was at various times an airplane pilot, artist, farmer, fencer, hunter, breeder of racehorses, polo player, collector of tropical fish, and shooter of wild animals in Africa. One felt he could do anything."[104]

OVERWHELMING DETERMINATION

So it is unrealistic for most of the rest of us mortals to think we could come anywhere near his prowess with language—or anything else. But he had his own handicaps. Although they were not as severe as those of many, they can be inspiring nonetheless. He fought determinedly to compensate for them and to fight against them, as it were.

We can be thankful that Winston did fight. For if historians are right, he was the critical factor that stymied the Nazi war machine just when it seemed invincible. And more precisely, it was his speeches that did more than anything else to steel British nerves when they were near collapse. How ironic that these speeches that helped turn the tide of history were given by a man who had a speech impediment.

Chapter 7

It's painful: Marilyn Monroe

> First time was at the orphanage, and then later in my teens I stuttered. And I was elected secretary of the minutes of the English class. . . . Then I'd say, [to announce] the minutes of the last meeting, I'd go m-m-m-m-m . . . Oh, it's terrible.
>
> —MARILYN MONROE[105]

Stuttering was the least of Marilyn Monroe's (1926–62) problems. She suffered through a lonely and traumatic childhood. Her father abandoned her mother before Marilyn was born; neither her mother, Gladys Baker, nor Marilyn were ever sure who her father was, because Gladys had had liaisons with four different men in the months around Marilyn's conception.[106] The young Marilyn, whose name for the first twenty years of her life was Norma Jeane, had three mothers in her first eight years because of Gladys's emotional problems. A year later she was sent to an orphanage, then two years later to a relative of one foster mother, and one year after that to yet another set of foster parents. When she was sixteen and her newest parents decided they could no longer afford to keep her, she got married to avoid being sent to an orphanage.

REJECTED BY HER MOTHER

Norma Jeane's first eight years were stable. Her foster parents were a Pentecostal couple who took her to church and warned her against the movies. But Norma Jeane never felt she could satisfy "Aunt Ida." As she put it years later, "It was hard to please them. Somehow I was always falling short, although I can't remember being especially bad."

But the worst pain in these first sixteen years was feeling rejected by her mother. "My mother didn't want me," Marilyn later recalled. Not only had Gladys given her up to foster parents shortly after her daughter's birth, but because of her mental distress drifted in and out of psychiatric hospitals for most of this time. Young Norma Jeane never knew when her mother would suddenly appear, and then just as suddenly disappear. It was such a strained relationship that in Marilyn's last ten years she refused to visit her mother, yet kept sending her money.

It is no wonder that Marilyn's life at many levels was a painfully insecure search for her identity. For most of her adult life, she tried to find it through work as an actress. But it was elusive. "As a person," she told an interviewer, "my work is important to me. My work is the only ground I've ever had to stand on. Acting is very important. To put it bluntly, I seem to have a whole superstructure with no foundation. But I'm working on the foundation."[107]

SEARCHING FOR A FATHER

She was also searching for the father she never had. This partly explains her three failed marriages. She was willing to marry James Dougherty not only to escape the orphanage but also because he was twenty-one and seemed to have the stability and maturity which she lacked. Joe DiMaggio attracted her because at thirty-seven and newly retired from the New York Yankees, his quiet and authoritative personality seemed to provide paternal protection and love. But when Joe beat her a second time for breaking her agreement not to wear revealing clothes in public, she divorced

him. She was persuaded that she could make up for her own ab-
breviated education (dropping out of school midway in her sopho-
more year of high school) by marrying playwright Arthur Miller,
but her discovery from his diary that she bored him brought that
marriage to an end as well.

MYSTERIOUS DEATH

Marilyn's accumulated insecurities and failed relationships drove
her eventually to addiction to pills—barbituates to get her to sleep
and then others to wake her up. They eventually led to her death,
which has puzzled investigators ever since. There was definitely
an overdose, but there were also strange, potentially poisonous,
elements found in her colon at the autopsy. Were they put in an
enema by a personal assistant who is reported to have given her
such intimate care? Was the overdose encouraged or managed
by Peter Lawford and the Kennedy brothers, with at least one of
whom it is certain she had an affair? Was she angry that the president never returned her calls after their intimate encounter, and
did she threaten to go public? Rumors have swirled for more than
a half-century, and while there is spotty evidence for each of these
theories and more, nothing is certain.[108]

THE FIRST TIME

For most of these tumultuous thirty-six years of life, Marilyn stuttered. It started when she was eight. A boarder in their home put
her on his lap and molested her. She ran to tell her mother, but
suddenly her tongue could not get the words out. "I want to tell
you something, about Mr. Kinnell. He . . . he . . . ."

Her mother interrupted her, and smacked her mouth. "Take
this for lying about a friend of mine. Don't you dare say anything
against Mr. Kinnell," Gladys screamed. "He's a fine man. He's my
star boarder."

Mr. Kinnell came into the room, handed Norma Jeane a nickel, and told her to buy herself an ice cream cone. She threw it in his face and ran out. Marilyn recalled that she cried herself to sleep that night.[109]

AT THE ORPHANAGE

The stammer got worse after she was sent to the orphanage. "The day they brought me there, after they pulled me in, crying and screaming, suddenly there I was in the large dining room with a hundred kids sitting there eating, and they were all staring at me. So I stopped crying right away [and] I stuttered." She says it got so bad that she could not finish her sentences.[110]

In 1955 she recalled, "I guess you might say I gave up talking for a long while. I used to be so embarrassed in school. I thought I'd die whenever a teacher called upon me. I always had the feeling of not wanting to open my mouth, that anything I said would be wrong or stupid."[111]

Apparently her speech got a little better for a while. But then, she recalled in 1960, "when I was about thirteen I took it [stuttering] up again. I don't know how it happened. I just stuttered."[112]

THE M-M-M-M GIRL

In ninth grade Norma Jean nearly failed Rhetoric and Spoken Arts because fear of speaking "paralyzed her throat and silenced her." Nevertheless, she was elected to be secretary of the minutes in the English class. But when she had to report on those minutes, she stammered on the words: "Then I'd say, [to announce] the minutes of the last meeting, I'd go m-m-m-m-m . . . Oh, it's terrible."[113] Her difficulty in pronouncing this word became so memorable that in her ninth-grade class of about five hundred students she was among the very few who were in the June 1941 printing of the class alphabet: " A for Ambitious: John Hurford . . . G for Glamorous:

Nancy Moon . . . R for Radical: Don Ball . . . V for Vivacious: Mary Jean Boyd . . . M-m-m-m: Norma Jeane Baker."[114]

When Norma Jeane was given her first screen test in Hollywood at the age of twenty, she began to stutter and perspire. To her great relief, she was told it was a silent test: she was to wear a floor-length crinoline gown, walk back and forth, sit on a high stool, light a cigarette, stub it out, and then walk toward a window. On the basis of that silent performance, she was given a contract with 20th Century Fox studios.

STUTTERING ON HER NAME

A month later she was told she would need a new name. Norma Jeane volunteered her mother's maiden name for a surname: Monroe. When Ben Lyon, a studio director, suggested "Jeane Monroe," the new actress said she wanted a complete change, and began to talk about her past. She had never known her father, her foster father had been abusive . . . and in high school she was known as the "Mmmmm Girl."

Lyon then blurted out, "I know who you are, you're Marilyn!" He explained that she reminded him of a lovely actress named Marilyn Miller.

When Lyon told her to pronounce her new name, she started to stutter again, "Mmmmmm . . ."

But then she gave herself a running start by starting with some other words. "Well, I guess I'm Marilyn Monroe."[115]

The stuttering continued. In an early student production at the Bliss-Hayden Miniature Theater, "she knew the dialogue perfectly, but she stuttered and paused so much that she threw the other student players into total confusion." As she went on to win roles in movies, she tended to stutter on the first takes on the set.[116]

But sometimes it was later takes as well. Her most famous line in the movie *Some Like It Hot*—"It's me, sugar"—took forty-seven takes before she got it right. Apparently Marilyn had the hardest time getting out the word "sugar."[117]

The problem persisted into her final days. It is reported that during the making of her final movie, the unfinished *Something's Got to Give*, she was under so much stress, not to mention the influence of drugs, that her stuttering returned with a vengeance. At times she could not deliver her lines at all.[118]

THE BREATHY VOICE

If stuttering was a recurring pattern in this troubled actress's life, how was she able to perform? How did she become such a famous movie star that people are now surprised to hear that she was a stutterer? The answer is not crystal clear, but there are strong clues.

We know that for many of her years in Hollywood Marilyn had an acting coach named Natasha Lytess, who taught the young actress to breathe and move her lips before she actually spoke. A focus on breathing helps many stutterers. But Natasha also instructed Marilyn to enunciate every syllable, especially final consonants. Marilyn practiced over and over such sentences as "I did not want to pet the dear, soft cat."[119]

This exaggerated diction might have helped distract Marilyn, as stutterers are sometimes helpfully distracted, from her problem with starting words. But at the same time the staccato style can produce a stopping and starting that makes it more likely the speaker will block on words starting with difficult consonants or vowels.

This is why it was probably Marilyn's "next drama coach"—unidentified in the Monroe biographies—who seems to have taught her how to speak with her now-legendary slow and breathy voice. This method helps most stutterers to move into difficult sounds without blocking on them. For "a breathy voice requires that the vocal cords remain somewhat open to permit the increased outflow of air associated with that voice quality. Open vocal cords are incompatible with locked vocal cords and engender fluent speech."[120] According to a stuttering therapist who has studied Marilyn's case, she used this "movie voice" whenever she entered a stressful situation.[121]

We also know that in the 1950s "breathy breathing" was a popular therapy among speech therapists. Charles Van Riper, for example, taught stutterers to slow down speech and prolong their words, and to use gentle breathing.[122]

Wherever she learned it, this method worked for Marilyn most of the time. She made many movies, and her stutter was never readily apparent once the movies got to the screen. Quite the contrary, in fact. Her breathy speech became famous, and is known today among speech therapists as a technique called the "Marilyn Monroe voice."[123] Most viewers have thought she was merely trying to be sexy. That might have been one reason, but her now-famous movie voice owed far more to her efforts to prevent stuttering.

A DUMB BLONDE?

If her movie voice made her sound sexy and helped prevent stuttering, it also had the unfortunate effect of making her sound dumb. In reality Marilyn was surprisingly intelligent. Director Henry Hathaway, "not known for his friendliness to actors," said that Marilyn was "marvelous to work with, very easy to direct and terrifically ambitious to do better. And *bright*, really bright. She may not have had an education, but she was naturally bright."[124]

Any reader will notice her depth in the letter she wrote to her psychoanalyst while recovering in a hospital after being locked up in a psychiatric ward at Payne-Whitney in New York City. The first two paragraphs are illustrative:

> Just now when I looked out the hospital window where the snow had covered everything suddenly everything is a kind of muted green. The grass, shabby evergreen bushes—though the trees give me a little hope—the desolate bare branches promising maybe there will be spring and maybe they promise hope.
>
> Did you see *The Misfits* [her most recent movie] yet? In one sequence you can perhaps see how bare and strange

a tree can be for me. I don't know if it comes across that way for sure on the screen—I don't like some of the selections in the takes they used. As I started to write this letter about four quiet tears had fallen. I don't know quite why.[125]

She went on to say that she was not able to sleep the previous night. So she "tried to be constructive about it and started to read the letters of Sigmund Freud." She wrote that she was struck by the sadness in his face in the opening photo.

He looked very depressed (which must have been taken near the end of his life) that he died a disappointed man—but Dr. Kris said he had much physical pain which I had known from the Jones book—but I know this too to be so but still I trust my instincts because I see a sad disappointment in his gentle face.[126]

HUMOR

Marilyn suffered through her own long bouts with melancholy throughout her adult life. But she was also full of humor, even in many of those depressed periods. When asked by a reporter if she had disrobed or played any other scenes of high drama at (the psych ward in) Payne-Whitney, she laughed.

"I only wish I had. It might have gotten something out of my system. But what I'm proud of is this: Just before I left there, I told all those doctors that they should have their heads examined." She giggled and then added, "I believe in psychiatry—but in a sane way."[127]

In better times she could be quick on her feet. After she had sung "Do It Again" at Camp Pendleton in 1952, the master of ceremonies bounced up on the stage to say she was the most beautiful sweater girl they had ever seen at this military base. Without a pause Marilyn turned to her audience of thousands of soldiers: "You fellows down there are always whistling at sweater girls. I don't get all the fuss. Take away the sweaters and what have you got?"

She was just as quick backstage. When a sassy journalist asked her if she was not wearing falsies, she replied, "Those who know me better, know better."[128]

When later that year she was leading the Miss America parade, she wore "a wispy black item with little here, less there, nothing much anywhere and a neckline that plunged to the waist and threatened to keep on going." Newspaper photographs angered church and women's groups all over the country. When asked about the commotion a few days later, Marilyn replied saucily, "People were staring down at me all day long, but I thought they were admiring my marshal's badge."[129]

Marilyn could turn even the pain of her own stuttering into a joke. In 1960 she told an interviewer about stuttering on a movie set.

> Sometimes if I'm very nervous or excited or something, I stutter. In fact, one time I had a small part in a movie and the assistant director came and yelled at me. Oh, he talked awful. So when I got into the scene, instead of my lines I [said], "Wo-wo-wo-wo . . . ." The director came up, he was furious, and said, "You don't stutter!!" I said, "That's what you think!"

But then Marilyn reminded herself and the interviewer that beneath the humor it hurts.

> "Oh, it's painful. Oh, God."[130]

Chapter 8

Historian and international lecturer:
Peter Brown

Peter Brown (1935–) has been called "one of the greatest humanists ever, and one of the best historians since the times of Herodotus and Thucydides."[131] His books on St. Augustine and late antiquity are landmarks in the field.[132] An eminent scholar nominating him for one of his many prizes wrote that "he is one of the very few scholars now alive who have, in effect, invented a field of study." For that field—late antiquity—"Brown's work provided the initiating Big Bang, in which he continues to function as a benevolent and generous Providence."[133]

Brown has won some of the world's most prestigious academic prizes—the Heineken Prize for History, the International Balzan Prize, and the Kluge Prize for Lifetime Achievement in the Study of Humanity, from the US Library of Congress.

He has taught at Oxford, Berkeley, and Princeton Universities. Many of the world's other great universities have awarded him honorary degrees.

Perhaps more astonishing for readers of this book, he is a distinguished public lecturer. He has been chosen to deliver named lectures such as the Carl Newell Jackson lectures at Harvard, and many other famous lecture series at other distinguished universities from Harvard, Chicago, Yale, and Stanford, to Cambridge, Oxford, and the British Academy.

Astonishing . . . because this famous lecturer still stutters, and sometimes noticeably so when he speaks—both privately and publicly. His story is a fascinating one.

CHILDHOOD: WALKING ON STILTS

Brown was born in Dublin, Ireland, to a Scotch-Irish Protestant family. I mention his religion because it was difficult then to be a Protestant in a city that was almost entirely Catholic. That didn't help matters when he was a boy struggling with a speech disability. People looked at him differently when he hesitated trying to get a word out, and then if they discovered he was a Protestant, it was a double whammy.

At first, he recalls, he did not think his stammering was a problem. But as he grew older it started to bother him. There were good days and bad days. "On a good day I was able to go to the shop for my aunt's pack of cigarettes and be able to place the order without needing to show the shopkeeper my aunt's note." On a bad day, "it locked me up."[134] He was able to speak only to his parents and aunt.

There was also the problem of "an invisible but crucial division between accents." Brown's family spoke with a slight English accent, which was picked up by their Irish neighbors and caused even more isolation for young Peter to suffer.

But Peter wasn't completely safe at home, either. "My mother was the product of a shame culture," so he grew up "fearing that she would feel ashamed" of his speech problem.

Yet she also tried to comfort her son. She would remind him often, "Don't worry, Peeds [Peter], the king has a stammer too." So George VI's speech problem (see chapter 5) was well-known then among the public, and helped young Peter not to feel totally alone. Nevertheless, he says now, "It was rare that one heard of other stammerers" in the 1940s.

Brown is a master of analogy. He compares these years of trying to be fluent to walking on stilts. He could do it for a while, but inevitably he came crashing down "to the ground of ordinary conversation" where his jaws ground to a halt. It was the "Antaeus complex," referring to the giant of Greek myth who would wrestle all passers-by and eventually crush them. Like the travelers in the myth, young Peter often felt that no matter how hard he wrestled with his adversary, defeat was inevitable.

He got some help when he was twelve from a nurse in Dublin who had some training in physiotherapy. She suggested he learn to breathe more slowly. "It did some good," he recalls.

But the defeats kept coming, if not as often. Brown remembers a time when he was thirteen, and traveling from Ireland to a Public School (private boarding school) at Shewsbury in England. He took a boat from Ireland to the Welsh coast, arriving at dawn. As he got off the boat, he tried to tell an imposing Welsh porter to take his trunk and put it on the right train. He tried and tried to say, "I am changing at Chester for Shrewsbury," but nothing came out. Eventually the kindly porter suggested, "Sing it, sonny." He knew that stutterers can sing what they cannot say.

As a teen Peter concluded that some professions were closed to him. "There was great respect for the verbal professions in those days—the teachers, the clergy, and lawyers. But these seemed to be closed doors because of my stammer. I remember feeling a sense of block to my life."

ADULT STRUGGLES: HANG GLIDING

When Brown finished graduate school at Oxford and started his academic career as a professor, Antaeus kept wrestling him. There was the daily tension of conversation with students and colleagues, wondering if he would block on a word, grasping for a substitute word that was easier to pronounce, but occasionally stumbling nonetheless. Brown's facility with language is legendary, so it was much easier for him than for most stutterers to think of another word that might do.

But there were still what the historian calls the "horrors." Those were the times in lecture when "I would have whole paragraphs in my head and could not get them out." It is every stutterer's nightmare—not only the frustration of not being able to express yourself but also a room full of anxious or impatient looks that make you want to crawl into a hole.

There were also the times outside of the lecture hall. The Princeton scholar remembers the time when he was on holiday in Greece with his wife. "I was already tense because it was a bad day for my speech. Then we were at a restaurant ordering our food, and I suddenly froze. I could barely utter a word. It was humiliating for me, and almost as frustrating for my wife."

The frustration still pops up. He still feels shame and anger when people laugh at him. "When I pick up prescriptions, for example, and can't get my name out, I have to mobilize all my limited capacity for Zen when someone giggles. Some cultures are worse than others. When it goes with ill will or dishonesty, it is unforgivable. But otherwise, I suppose, I should see it as an embarrassed reaction—like the Japanese ambassadors who (I am told) giggled with shame when confronted by Cordell Hull with the news of Pearl Harbor."

Since Professor Brown is a scholar whose interface with the world is through his books and lectures, the lecture hall is where Antaeus most regularly stalks him. He says he has come to regard the public lecture as a form of hang gliding. "As I speak in front of a classroom or crowd, I am constantly looking for the proper language to communicate my meaning, but words that will not trip me up. It's like a hang-glider that must be carefully directed to find updrafts and avoid downdrafts, and be sure not to land where it would wreck."

It's an exhilarating but dangerous game. Brown knows he has stories to tell that no other scholar can tell, and the opportunity to open past worlds to new audiences can be energizing. But there are great hazards. In this sense, he says, it sometimes feels like "getting chased down a narrow alley by a mugger. One has to be fast and skillful to escape."

He recalls one time when the mugger got to him. It had been a gray winter, and he had been depressed. He was returning that year on a half-time basis because he was fearful of a stroke (a medical condition that has now disappeared). This was a cocktail reception for junior faculty. Brown, a senior professor, was eagerly sought out by the young professors who wanted advice on how to be a scholar and teach and have a private life as well.

Brown looked forward to the occasion. He is known for his generosity to younger scholars. But on this late afternoon that winter, he blocked repeatedly on words. He just could not get his words out. Antaeus had wrestled him to the ground again with what he calls "that terrible awkwardness."

ZEST AND STRATEGIES

But all is not gloom and doom. Far from it. Peter Brown is a jovial fellow with a twinkle in his eyes. He is warm and gregarious. He does not let Antaeus keep him from living life with zest. If he gets wrestled to the ground and feels crushed on a given day, he gets up the next day knowing that not every day will be like yesterday.

"I have a zest for languages," he tells us. "I love learning, speaking, and hearing them." Even if speaking English or other languages is sometimes a chore, the mere engagement with words in all their varieties brings him joy.

But especially the written word. "Writing has always given me freedom to make my own choices, to use words that perfectly communicate the nuances of meaning that I could never utter aloud." It is as if writing provides Brown the full release—emotionally and intellectually—that is never fully possible for a stutterer. Although he enjoys the high-wire act that is public speaking, writing brings the special pleasure of being able to get the words just right.

Now that he is teaching beyond the normal retirement age, he has advice for younger stutterers. First, he advises, "they should know that verbal smartness is not enough." Just having the most clever words in your head will not cut it. You must have strategies, you must think through your speaking situations, especially if you are called to speak in public.

Realize, he warns, that it won't be easy. "I have gray hair and a thick skin to prove it." Over the years he came to see that blowing it in public hurts, but it is not the end of the world. It is painful, but you learn that there is always another day, and you can learn strategies.

"For example, there is always a hiatus between the written text and what language really is—a set of social gestures with appropriate noises." He advises students and young professors to always bring a written text, but not to follow it religiously. "The text is not your talk. Use the text as a basic script that you can adapt as you go along, by departing from it here and there and being spontaneous."

Brown does this when he lectures in public. He marks every five-minute break in his text, where he feels free to become spontaneous, elaborating on a point or saying something he had not previously planned. "I do this not to avoid stuttering per se, but because I value enormously being unself-conscious. That is a virtue in itself. And when I am being unself-conscious, it so happens that I stutter less."

Brown reads more than fifteen languages and speaks ten. No one can follow his next piece of advice as well as he, but to those stutterers who know more than one language he suggests they use other languages to get them through when English fails them. He used his knowledge of French and Gothic languages when travelling through France and unable to get an English word out. "Trying another language can provide the distraction one needs to slip through a block." Cold phone calls have always been very hard for him, as they are for most stutterers, but he found they were easier when he used another language. He suggests that young teachers who struggle use a foreign language to open their talks, since the beginning is often the toughest part of an oral address. Once the speaker gets started, it usually gets easier.

The important thing is to get your voice working somehow, he suggests, not the precise words. Let your imagination work once you start, using whatever words come to you to get the ball rolling.

He also has advice about the dynamics in a social setting. "I wish someone had told me early on that my speech will impact others. My stammering will sometimes make others feel uncomfortable." So Brown learned ways to put his audiences at ease. "Sometimes I say, 'I'm sorry I have a stammer.'"

"Or I use humor. Recently I was speaking at Rutgers [University]. When I started to stammer, I stopped and said, 'Sorry. It must be the jet lag from Princeton.'" It is a 25-minute drive between the two campuses.

LEARNING FROM A DISABILITY

Peter Brown has learned more from late antiquity and the early middle ages than anyone else on the planet. He has also learned from his battles with his tongue.

First, he says, "It gave me a zest for writing. The oral word came hard, and was off-putting. So I came to the written word, which was easy and delightful. It opened up to me the whole world. Then I discovered the extraordinary worlds of literature. And from there, it was not too long before I discovered that I could communicate with my own words on paper in ways that were liberating."

Like many stutterers, Brown was drawn to reading and writing. In fact, his stuttering might have hastened his immersion in the literary world, and thus helped produce this remarkable humanist.

Brown says his stammer also made him compassionate. He had suffered for many years, and so his heart went out to others who were obviously suffering. As a professor in the classroom, he tended to give favor to the shy students. He remembered the years when he was one of them, often misunderstood because he did not speak much.

Finally, he suggests intriguingly, stuttering can open one to transcendence. "Sometimes we stutter for good reason. Perhaps we are not getting on well. There is something we should be searching for, but we're not. We should be allowing ourselves to be bored, but instead we get immersed in mundane pleasures.

"Stuttering can come from our wonder that there must be more. It can provide a moment of transcendence, and that is liberating."

Chapter 9

Award-winning TV journalist:
John Stossel

John Stossel (1947–) is a familiar face to millions of Americans. For decades he was a correspondent on ABC's *20/20* and consumer reporter for *Good Morning America.* His "Give Me a Break" segments took skeptical looks at everything from government regulations and pop culture to censorship and unfounded fears. Since 2009 he has hosted a weekly news show on Fox Business, *Stossel*, and now appears weekly on *The O'Reilly Factor.*

Stossel nearly crashed and burned at his first TV news job in Portland. He had been doing prerecorded stories that could be edited if he stuttered. One day he was asked to replace an anchorman for a live five-minute newscast, and he reluctantly agreed. When he had to read the script about what candidates for city council had spent in their election campaigns, there was no way to avoid the "d" sound that had always troubled him. "John Smith," he started, "spent one hundred thousand . . . . d-d-d-d-d-d-dollars." Stossel was blocking so badly that the sound engineer cut him off the air before he could go further. "I was utterly humiliated."[135]

I CAN'T

Stossel never intended to go into TV news. His stuttering was humiliating at times, but never very severe. He says he would have lived with it if he had not gone into TV. When he was an undergraduate at Princeton, he was fairly successful at hiding it, by substituting words and avoiding talking in certain situations.

When he graduated, he took a job with *Seattle Magazine* as a writer even though he hated English classes and never took a class in journalism. "They offered to pay my way to the Pacific Northwest. Since it was the longest free trip I was ever offered, I took it."

By the time Stossel arrived in Seattle, the magazine had gone out of business. The parent company offered him a job as a researcher in its Portland, Oregon TV newsroom.

After researching and writing stories for the TV anchor for two years, the anchor asked if he wanted to do his own reporting on air. "I can't," he told them. "I'm a stutterer."

"Oh, you're not that bad," he was told. "Try it."

Stossel did, and found he could do it. "When I am pushed, I—like other moderate stutterers—can act." It went all right for a while. He occasionally blocked on a word, but since his stories were all taped, the editor simply snipped out those sentences, and Stossel did those parts over.

Then came the time he was asked to fill in for the anchorman, when he was cut off the air in mid-sentence, and he suddenly reverted to the shame and fear of his childhood.

TERRIBLY ASHAMED

"As a boy, I stuttered on plosive sounds." These are the hard consonants like "p," "b," and "d," where the vocal tract is blocked and airflow stops. Stossel says he dealt with it by retreating into the closet: "My main remedy was not to talk or to substitute a synonym. Or I would distract myself until I could get the word out. But usually, I simply was quiet. I chose not to speak up in class, because I was always terribly ashamed."

His parents sent him to speech therapists at Northwestern University during the school year, and to speech camps during the summer run by the University of Michigan. At these camps there were children who had speech problems because they were deaf, or had cleft palates or cerebral palsy. "The stutterers and cerebral palsy kids stuck together."

The camps lasted for eight weeks. By the end of each summer, Stossel says he spoke "pretty well." But after two or three weeks back home, he relapsed.

"None of these therapies did much good after a while."

I HATED IT

"But I did what I could, using what I had been taught. In those days speech therapists told their clients to use 'light contact.' This meant hitting each sound more gradually."

This worked for Stossel, up to a point.

"I was still a closet stutterer, trying to hide it. It became a habit not to reach out or take risks. I would always consult the map and not ask for directions, for example. Or I would not ask for things at the store, but find things on my own."

At the same time, Stossel knew he couldn't hide completely. Therapists in those days told stutterers to go out in public and deliberately try to speak with strangers. The idea was that stuttering was caused by fear, and that speaking enough to strangers would beat the fear by desensitizing stutterers to such public encounters.

But it didn't work for Stossel. "I hated it. And what's more, it didn't desensitize me. Blocking in public kept making me feel ashamed."

So he continued to try to hide.

"I envied those stutterers who were less self-conscious. They were the wiser for it, and happier."

Stossel points to Jack Welch, the legendary CEO of General Electric. Welch was asked how he ran an enormous company with a rather severe stutter. Welch's answer was, "I don't give a shit. I just stutter."

Stossel wished he could have had that level of self-confidence. "Closet stutterers are the worst. They live in fear of blocking in public." It didn't make it any easier to see those more self-confident stutterers in action. They usually did something to distract themselves, like punching their leg or flailing their arms or developing a facial tic.

"The problem with letting yourself do that is that after a while it doesn't work anymore, and you have to add something. Then you start looking grotesque. I could not do that."

THE BREAKING POINT

Stossel struggled on, trying to hide his problem as best he could.

But then came the night when he was cut off the air at the TV station in Portland. He was humiliated, but his boss was less bothered than he was. "He told me to hang in there and keep trying."

So he did. Occasionally he had to anchor again. "I was good at substituting synonyms and acting. I was actually pretty fluent. In conversation I had better days and worse days."

Then Stossel got a job at WCBS-TV in New York City as a consumer reporter. For a few years he did pretty well, holding the stuttering demon at bay.

But the stuttering came back.

"I would produce a story that lasted three to five minutes, and be able to edit my blocks out. But at the end of the story I had to go live, and do chit-chat with the anchor for about twenty seconds.

"I would wake up every morning scared. By 6 PM I had been a nervous wreck all day, dreading a future humiliation.

"It almost never came, but the fear was a hundred times worse than the rare stutter. The whole pattern of working and dreading what might or might not happen was self-destructive.

"I was miserable, and ready to quit."

Then a therapist suggested he try a three-week program at the Hollins Communications Research Institute in Roanoke, Virginia.

Stossel went. It was 1978. He says that after all the failed therapies he had endured, he had no confidence this would work. But he was also desperate, and so permitted himself to hope.

HOLLINS

The first two weeks of therapy at Hollins taught Stossel how to pronounce each sound slowly and gently. This therapy had developed from a hypothesis conceived some years before by its founder, psychologist Ronald Webster.

Some speech therapies before that time were based on the assumption that stuttering was an emotional problem. Stutterers had been traumatized, it was thought, by something in childhood that produced fear. That fear would contract the vocal cords, which then would stiffen and freeze, producing the block at the heart of stuttering. So the aim of those therapies was to either go back to those childhood events and try to defuse the fear by confronting it at its origin, or teach stutterers how to counteract the results of the fear by relaxing when they spoke in difficult situations. Cure rates were low. While many stutterers found effective help through a variety of other therapies, stutterers like Stossel spent time and money without much to show for their efforts.

Webster was not convinced that stuttering was caused by emotional problems. He noticed that many stutterers were quite healthy emotionally, and many non-stutterers had emotional problems. He also reasoned that just because nervousness can provoke or aggravate a stutter does not mean that stuttering is *caused* by nerves. Many other conditions are aggravated by nerves without being caused by nerves, such as Miniere's disease, irritable bowel syndrome, migraines, and some heart disease. Each of these is said to be triggered or heightened when their sufferers are under stress. But none is believed to be *caused* by emotional stress.

Webster hypothesized that stuttering was caused by a neurophysiological defect, not emotional disorder. If that were true, he reasoned, then stutterers probably would behave *physically* in ways non-stutterers don't. Perhaps when stutterers spoke fluently, they were nevertheless breathing and moving their vocal cords and associated muscles in ways fundamentally different from the ways non-stutterers breathe and move those muscles.

To test his hypothesis, Webster first studied *non*-stutterers, measuring precisely in controlled experiments how they breathed and used the muscles and nerves that produce speech. Then he used the same precise measurements on *stutterers* to determine how they breathed and used these muscles and nerves and their voice box *when they were speaking fluently.*

The results were astonishing. Just as he had guessed, the stutterers were breathing and using their larynx and jaw muscles differently from non-stutterers even when they were fluent.

So the solution seemed simple in theory—even if difficult in practice. He would need to teach stutterers how to breathe and move their speech muscles in the same way non-stutterers breathe and move their speech muscles.

Stuttering, Webster reasoned, must be a learned pattern of physical movement involving the lungs and lips and jaw muscles. In a word, it seemed to be a bad habit.

Bad habits are hard to break. But they can be broken, if replaced by new habits.

Webster had to teach stutterers new habits of moving these parts of their bodies.

All this sounded marvelous. But would it work?

ECSTASY

For the first two weeks Stossel was taught to spend two whole seconds on each syllable. He had to repeat the sound precisely, starting the sound with gentle onset, into a computer listening device that would register "Yes" only if Stossel did it precisely right. If he made the sound with even the slightest imprecision, an ugly sound pierced the air, and he didn't get "credit." He had to do it right over and over, with an immense variety of practice exercises, so that by the end of the two weeks he had pronounced each sound correctly at least three thousand times. This was what it took, according to Webster's research, for a new habit to be formed. After this point, the stutterer would have new "muscle memory" that would kick in with little or no thinking. It would be nearly automatic.

Stossel could hardly believe it, but by the end of the first two weeks it was working to a degree that no therapy had ever helped before. The third week brought the test. He and his fellow stutterers were sent out to shopping malls to speak to strangers.

It was frightening at first, but it worked. Stossel was amazed.

"I was ecstatic! I was so thrilled that I could finally say sounds that were always so hard, that they couldn't shut me up. It was like a cork being taken out of a bottle of champagne."

LIFELONG PRACTICE

He returned home jubilantly. Life would never be the same, he thought. His career might change, now that he could speak freely and didn't have to live in fear.

But then disaster struck anew. Two days later he was on a bus, practicing with strangers. Suddenly the old nemesis returned. He stuttered, and seemed to be relapsing into his old bad habits.

"I was heartbroken." He called Catherine, the therapist who had trained him at Hollins. She told him not to be shocked. It simply meant that he had to keep practicing what he had been taught at Hollins. "You might have to practice all your life."

SUCCESS

He did practice, and diligently. He remembers that two years after his Hollins therapy he continued to practice in public.

"I reached the point where I didn't mind annoying people. My wife still remembers going with me into a store where I asked for millets. Now I didn't even know what millets were, and wouldn't know what to do with them if they had sold me some.

"It was humiliating to practice like that, but it helped. Gradually I got better and better. Now I stutter occasionally, but it is rare."

Stossel did some stories on people who were trained at Hollins, and found that not everyone was as transformed as he was. The older ones had a harder time because their habits were more deeply ingrained. The old adage is true: it is hard to teach an old dog new tricks.

"But maybe another reason I got so much better is that I was so motivated." He knew his career depended on it. He needed it every day.

His practice was easier because his job provided the perfect opportunity to use the Hollins principles daily. "Speaking on TV automatically slows you down and makes you think about your sounds." These are part of the Hollins training—to speak more slowly and to think about breathing and gentle onsets so that each sound is pronounced correctly.

It worked. Stossel rose to the top of his profession. As a reporter he won nineteen Emmy Awards and was honored five times for excellence in consumer reporting by the National Press Club.

MAINTENANCE

Stossel maintains fluency by practicing with one of his doormen in the building where he lives in Manhattan. The doorman is a stutterer, but Stossel helped him go through the Hollins program, and the two remind each other to stay "on target."

"His mere presence is a reminder to me. I practice a few difficult words each day, and when I walk by him, I stop and practice them with him. That probably helps."

I asked Stossel if he is ever afraid now. "Occasionally, but rarely. Sometimes when I am on *O'Reilly*. I dread certain sounds, and am relieved if they come out smoothly."

Sometimes, he says, he just goes ahead and stutters on air to prove to himself it is not that bad. "I keep thinking about Jack Welch not being hung up by his stuttering. And when I do actually stutter, it's never that terrible."

Today it's not terrible because it is so rare. Stossel says it happens only once every couple of years.

THANK YOU, STUTTERING

Looking back, Stossel can see three ways that stuttering helped make him successful. The first was that it helped him find his niche. Because he stuttered, he never sought the higher-paying TV anchor job where you had to speak live so much. He also didn't want to be the typical reporter who had to shout out questions to a politician at a news conference or press briefing.

So he became a consumer reporter when there were no others. He worked harder on research and background to find what no one else was finding because they were at the news conferences. In the process, he discovered that these background stories were more interesting anyway.

"Most TV news is about politics, crime, and the weather. It's absurdly shallow and narrow-minded. Most of what politicians do—even senators—doesn't affect people very much.

"What is important usually happens slowly, away from state capitols—things like the development of the computer chip, the women's movement, segregation. Things work gradually—and so don't get reported in most TV news—in science, ecology, the economy, and religion.

"So my digging deeper to get at these more gradual changes that affect ordinary lives made me stand out."

Stuttering also taught him something about words, which of course are at the heart of what he does for a living. "Because I was afraid to speak for so long, I gradually came to appreciate the value of words, and the need for economy with words. I came to conclude that it is usually best to use fewer words, and not waste people's time."

Stossel learned to be brief and to speak more simply—very helpful when TV stories are measured not only in minutes but seconds.

A third lesson that stuttering taught Stossel was that you can be more original when you're not in the mainstream.

Speech pathology, he claims, is a huge industry that until recently helped very few people. It labored for a long time under what he calls "self-delusion." It claimed to be of use when it really was not.

(I should add that many disagree at this point. Speech therapists work successfully on many speech problems other than stuttering. And there are many stutterers who say they have received much help from various speech therapy techniques, not just now but also in decades past. See, for example, Judith Kuster, "Voices: Past and Present" [https://www.mnsu.edu/.comdis/voices/voiccs.html] or *Advice to Those Who Stutter* from the Stuttering Foundation.)

Now back to Stossel: Think of Lionel Logue, the therapist in *The King's Speech* [chapter 5]. He was unlicensed and unapproved by the experts of his day. Speech therapy didn't improve until it learned from the novel techniques he developed on his own.

"When anesthesiology was first invented, the best surgeons opposed it. They prided themselves on how quickly they could perform a procedure because speed was a premium when there were no pain-killers. These speedy surgeons said to themselves, 'If anesthesia is widely used, then any idiot will be able to operate!'

"Einstein was never associated with a major university until the last part of his career. When he was developing his greatest theories of relativity, he was a patent clerk—away from the scientific establishment. This gave him more freedom to think for himself, and come up with original ideas."

So Stossel does not lament his many years of struggle with this handicap. He sees that it played a role in making him as successful as he is. If many have begun to think differently on a host of issues that Stossel has discussed on TV and in his three books—such as government and the free market, and other libertarian ideas—then they have his stuttering to thank.

Chapter 10

Astronaut's wife with the right stuff: Annie Glenn

Both John Glenn and his wife Annie (1920–) broke the sound barrier. John did it in 1957 when he was the first person to fly a jet across the country at supersonic speed—in three hours and thirty-two minutes, which was faster than a bullet fired from a .45 caliber pistol.[136]

Annie did it when she was fifty-three years old. After a life of being afraid to answer the telephone and unable to call the plumber or order a meal, she suddenly became able to give speeches. When she first called her husband announcing her breakthrough, he wept.

THE MOVIE

Most Americans remember Annie Glenn's stuttering from *The Right Stuff*, the 1983 movie adapted from Tom Wolfe's best-selling 1979 book of the same title about the test pilots who were selected to be the astronauts for Project Mercury, the first attempt at manned spaceflight by the United States. John Glenn was one of these seven astronauts, and became the first American to orbit the earth.

In one unforgettable scene from the movie, reporters are pushing through the bushes and looking into the windows of the

Glenn home in Arlington, Virginia, while the nation is waiting for John's rocket to blast off. The flight had just been cancelled again, after several false starts, this time because of weather.

Vice president Lyndon Baines Johnson is in a black limousine outside, demanding that Annie let him into the house with TV cameras.

"Tell her I'd like to pay her a sympathy call," he orders an aide.

When the aide relays the message through a window to one of Annie's friends, huddled with her inside, Annie responds with an emphatic "No."

She knows that she would be asked for a comment on nation-wide TV, and that she would be unable to get a word out.

Johnson refuses to take no for an answer. "Get somebody to tell her to play ball."

NASA officials tell John, who has just come down from the rocket, that his wife has a serious problem. John picks up a phone that NASA had patched in to Annie.

"Annie, it's me. Tell me what's wrong."

"J-J-Johnson w-w-w-ants m-m-e on [pause] TV."

A NASA official, overhearing what Annie said to John, urges, "It's important, John."

John bites his lip, and tells Annie in a raised voice so the NASA official can hear, "Listen to me. If you don't want the vice president or the TV networks or anybody else, then that's it. I'll back you up all the way 100 percent on this."

Raising his voice even more, John shouted, "You tell them the astronaut John Glenn told you to say that!"

The scene ends with a shot of the limo rocking back and forth at the curb, as Johnson explodes inside in a temper tantrum.

"Isn't there anybody who can deal with a housewife?" he screams.

Annie says today that the movie didn't have all the right stuff. She was actually in bed because of a migraine headache. And she adds that years later Johnson and his wife came to the Glenn home for dinner.[137]

CHILDHOOD SWEETHEARTS

Anna Margaret Castor and John Glenn met in a playpen. Their parents knew each other, and the two children became playmates first, and then high school sweethearts.

Annie says it was a happy childhood.

"I never realized I had a problem until the end of sixth grade, when I had to recite a poem and people laughed. My father was the town dentist. He too stuttered, but that never stopped him from anything. He was very active in town. So I didn't think that a speech difficulty was unusual.

"Of course, I knew that I didn't talk, but I was accepted. People just thought of me as quiet. I had lots of friends. Living in a small college town helped."

TORTURE

But things changed when Annie got older. She and John went to Muskingum College in Ohio, where she majored in music, and excelled on the organ. By the time she was a senior, she was so accomplished on the organ that the Juilliard School in New York City offered her a scholarship to do graduate study. But neither she nor John thought she would survive in the city because of her stutter. As John puts it,

> Shopping in an unfamiliar store was torture. She had to write a description of what she wanted, or take a sample to show a clerk, because she couldn't ask for it. Without those aids, she had to hunt all over the store, and sometimes she simply went home in frustration. People often laughed at her as she tried to get the words out.[138]

The war intervened. In the summer of 1942, after Annie had graduated and John finished junior year, John started training to be a Navy fighter pilot. He would go on to fly fifty-nine combat missions in World War II and another ninety in Korea. So Annie became a military wife, which meant many moves to new Marine bases, where she had to make new friends in new situations. This is usually a nightmare for stutterers, and Annie at this point was stuttering on 85 percent of her words.

"It was hard, but I made things work. It takes time to make new friends, but I have always loved meeting new people, and I did even then. Most of the time I was accepted for who I was—quiet. I always had lots of friends. I was never lonely.

"But yes, it was often frustrating. Can you imagine how frustrating it is not being able to say hello?

"I would discipline my kids with my hand and my eyes. When I had to take a child to the doctor or emergency room, I tried to take a friend with me to talk for me.

"But I worried. What if I couldn't find someone? What if it were an emergency, and I couldn't find the words to get the information across on the phone?

"Sometimes it was humiliating. There were sales people at stores who would write notes back to me, thinking I was deaf. Some would even circle their finger in the air, as if to say 'she's crazy.'

"There were also clerks who would interrupt me while I was trying to get a word out—'Lady, I don't have all day!'

"John was always my best friend and help when he was home. He would make calls to repairmen and friends when I needed him to."

COURAGE

It took courage for Annie to move to a new base, over and over during John's military career. Then after the Korean War, John became a test pilot and eventually an astronaut. Again, there were moves from place to place. Annie endured it all with good cheer, despite her stutter, and despite the fears of losing her husband.

They had a ritual. Every time John was deployed to a new military assignment, or was about to leave for another dangerous mission, his last words to her were, "I'm just going down to the corner store to get a pack of gum."

If she was the only person with him (if others were near, she would not be able to get the words out), she would always reply, "Don't be long."

On that famous day in February 1962 when he left to board the rocket that would hurtle him into outer space, with the whole nation watching anxiously, John and Annie said the same words.

But this time John gave her a packet of gum before he left, and she clutched it tightly until he had returned safely.

When it appeared that the heat shield on John's space capsule might come off during re-entry, NASA relayed news of the danger to Annie. "I waited for you to come back on the radio," she told him by phone after he had been hauled up onto an aircraft carrier in the Atlantic Ocean.

"I know it was only five minutes. But it seemed like five years."[139]

John has been called one of America's greatest heroes, and he has been hailed for his courage. But he says Annie's courage has been greater.

"I saw Annie's perseverance and strength through the years and it just made me admire her and love her even more." He says he has heard the ovation of thousands over the years, but he cheers far more for his wife and her accomplishments: "I don't know if I would have had the courage."[140]

BREAKTHROUGH

Like most stutterers, Annie was subjected to many speech therapists and programs to try to help her. None worked. As John puts it, "They had functioned primarily as feel-good sessions; they eased the psychological burdens of stuttering, but didn't solve the problem."[141]

Then one morning in 1973 John and Annie were watching the *Today* show when a guest appeared from a small college in Virginia. Ronald Webster was a psychology professor at Hollins College, where he had developed a remarkably successful program to help stutterers. (This is the same program described in the previous chapter on John Stossel.)

"Annie," John said to his wife, "this sounds like what we've been hunting for."

Several months later Annie was in the program in Roanoke.

"It was very intense. Three weeks, and eleven hours of work each day. No one from our families could call us. I was in a room alone. But I made friends, of course, with the others who were there in the program."

At the end of the three weeks, Annie called John. He says he will never forget that call.

"John," she said very carefully and slowly, "today we went to a shopping center and went shopping. And I could ask for things! Imagine that."

John had never before heard Annie speak so many words without a single pause. He says he knelt down to say a prayer of thanks.

When Annie got home, she had a surprise for John.

With a grin on her face she said, "John, I've wanted to tell you this for years: Pick up your socks."

John says the phone bills went up because Annie started calling friends all over the country. She told him she felt like a butterfly that had been let out of a cage.[142]

LIKE A DREAM

That was forty years ago. Annie's life since then has been even more full than it was as a mother and Marine/pilot/astronaut/senator's wife.

"I have loved making speeches ever since. Scout's honor. I love meeting people and talking, and being able to talk so much more freely has meant that I have been able to be even more involved than before. I love it all.

"When John was a senator, I asked my friend Rene Carpenter to come with me as I went around and made speeches. Then in 1984, when John was running for the Democratic presidential nomination, I made a lot of speeches again. I really did enjoy it.

"Even better, maybe, is that I have been able to shop more, and not be afraid. I cannot tell you what a relief it is to be able to ask where something is, and not have to hunt and hunt all over a store."

But Annie says the best part of her new life is that she can help people more.

"I have become known a bit for having battled with stuttering," she says modestly.

"So people from all over the country ask me for help. And I want to be of help. I stay in contact with as many as I can, and try to help them through their struggles.

"Isn't it wonderful to be able to help people?"

But there are still struggles. Annie still stutters some, and she speaks with a bit of halting.

And her stuttering has caused some disappointments along the way, even since her breakthrough. In 1980, for example, when Jimmy Carter was looking for a vice presidential candidate, Rosalyn reportedly decided after an interview with the Glenns that Annie's stutter would be an obstacle to the campaign. Carter decided eventually on Walter Mondale. John says, "It shocked us and it hurt."[143]

Annie says she no longer hides her stutter. She no longer keeps quiet out of fear. But she still has problems with words that start with "H." She says she needs to practice more what she learned at Hollins.

She keeps a sign by her phone that reads, "Full breath, relax your throat, keep the sound moving."

But what is striking about Annie is that she has always refused to let stuttering define her. When I asked her if her breakthrough has made her happier, she insisted she has always been happy—because of her love for people, support from her family, and her faith.

No doubt her excellent health has had something to do with that happiness. And her athletic determination has helped keep her healthy. She was a star swimmer in high school, has always loved tennis, and has skied until very recently—when she was past ninety.

"I had my knees operated on recently, and my surgeon tells me I can't ski for a while. But John and I keep hiking. We always have. We hike in the mountains near Vail, and we have always taken long walks together."

Perhaps the other key to Annie's sunny disposition, and no doubt to John's great successes, has been their marriage.

"We're going on seventy-two years of marriage," she tells me. "Do you think it will last?"

Annie says they have never had a fight. "We have argued, of course."

So what has been their secret to such a happy marriage?

"We are very open with each other—honest and trusting. We also find each other so comfortable, like a pair of old shoes. We enjoy the same movies, the same things on TV, and most of all, doing things together."

Annie says that life since her breakthrough forty years ago has been "like a dream."

But then Annie's life even before her breakthrough—even when she endured the torture of stuttering on 85 percent of her words—was something of a dream. She was happy then, and had plenty of friends then, and had a wonderful marriage and family then—despite the agony.

Perhaps the moral of her story is that while a breakthrough in speech can be like a dream, there is more to the dream of life than our speech.

Chapter 11

ABC News correspondent: Byron Pitts

When Byron Pitts (1960–) was in fifth grade, a therapist announced to his startled parents that their son was "functionally illiterate." He had hidden his problem by getting other students to read to him and then memorizing enough to get by.

Another supposed expert suggested to Byron's mother that he was mentally retarded.

Part of the reason for this was Byron's silence most of the time, which was a strategy to hide his other problem, stuttering. He wanted so badly to speak—to tell his parents to stop fighting, to stand up to the bully who taunted him, or simply to ask for a lemonade at school—but he couldn't get the words out. It was torture. It felt, he recalls, "like living as a prisoner inside a cell."[144]

Both of these problems, illiteracy and stuttering, caused him to hang his head in shame. The embarrassment and shame filled him with anger toward himself, and sensitivity to the slightest insult.

Yet this boy who could not read until he was eleven, and who stuttered painfully until he was twenty, went on to become an Emmy Award-winning journalist and correspondent for *60 Minutes*.

"WHAT DID I DO?"

One of the worst moments of Pitts's difficult childhood was getting caught—literally—between his parents in their last fight before their divorce. His father, William, was discovered by his wife Clarice in the home of one of his many paramours.

Clarice threatened to set his car on fire if he didn't come out of the house.

Out he came.

Clarice ordered nine-year-old Byron into his father's car. Then she threw brick after brick at her husband's head, as her husband bobbed and weaved. Every brick missed, as the neighbors watched in laughter.

When William finally managed to jump into his car, he failed to close the door. Clarice jumped in after him, and proceeded to scratch at his eyes and face, cursing all the while. William's head somehow wound up on Byron's lap, so the blood from his father's face ran onto his white shirt.

Byron screamed in terror. "Why? What did I do? Wha-wa-wa-wut!!"

He had more to stay, but couldn't get past the word *what*. He was tongue-tied even here, with his own parents, at one of the most critical times of their lives—and his.

A WARM SPIRITUAL BATH

Church was almost his only escape from his parents' fighting and his own torments. Like most stutterers, Byron discovered that when he sang his tongue was never bound. He started a lifetime of singing in church choirs. The music itself was liberating at New Shiloh Baptist Church.

"I'm sometimes up! I'm sometimes down! Almost leveled to the ground, but I'll keep on holding on!" This and countless other hymns spoke to Byron's soul.

No matter what happened at school or at home, Pitts found healing at church. Others might find joy and peace at the beach, but he agreed with his mother that the church was the poor man's therapy session. As one of his pastors put it, church was "a warm spiritual bath."

It didn't hurt that his church was led by a legendary black preacher, Rev. Harold A. Carter. "He could hoot with the best of them. Sweat profusely on the coldest days. Draw out the name Jesus the length of the Great Wall of China. I could listen to that man read the words on a can of paint."[145]

Byron left church most Sundays with a message that lifted him up, giving him the strength to endure another week of frustration and shame.

SIT DOWN AND SHUT UP

He was one of "the basement boys." After he was diagnosed as functionally illiterate, Byron was sent to the basement of St. Katharine's Catholic School for remedial reading classes. Each morning those who could read at grade level marched upstairs, but Byron and others trudged downstairs for the day.

"I could sometimes hear the whispers of pity or contempt. 'There go the dummies, fresh off the short bus.'"[146]

Furniture and equipment were spare down there, and so was the teaching. Most classes started with "Sit down and shut up!" Teaching was done in groups, not with individuals. There was usually no homework. Most were boys. If there was a fight in the morning, they would spend the whole day in a darkened classroom.[147]

Pitts wanted to learn to read, but not so that he could actually read. He simply wanted to give his mother a reason not to be ashamed. And to finally have a way to stop other kids making fun of him.

But by sixth grade Byron was still struggling. One day while watching TV, he saw a commercial for a reading program for adults who cannot read. When his mother came home from work, he announced hopefully, "Momma, if they can teach adults to read, then maybe it's not too late for me."[148]

In a few days a man dropped off a reading machine at their house and showed them how to use it. It used phonics, the classic method that teaches how to sound out each letter.

"What I should have learned at age four, I was finally getting at age eleven."

But it wasn't easy. There were tears and despair. One day he cried out, "I'm almost in high school, and I'm studying the alphabet? I really am a moron. People will laugh at me. I'll never catch up."

Finally, after much dogged hard work, Byron brought home a teacher's note and did what he had never been able to do before: read it out loud to his mother. Slowly he pronounced the words, "Mrs. Pitts, Byron is doing better in school. He is showing real pro . . . pro . . . progress."

For the first time, Byron and Clarice cried together.

WITH THE DUMMIES AGAIN

But the shame didn't end, at least not for a while. Byron could now read, but still very slowly. When he entered Archbishop Curley High School, he was ranked 310 out of 330 students. Once again he was assigned to a remedial reading class. And once again it was called the class for dummies.

But instead of feeling inferior, Byron used anger to get through. "I hated anyone who was smarter than I was," which meant almost all of his classmates in freshman year. The anger somehow made it easier to function. He took his mother's advice to kill them all with kindness, and work twice as hard as they did. So he was slow to comprehend words on a page, but was also called by his teachers the *most polite boy in class* and *the hardest worker we've ever seen.*[149] But with all that hard work, he still got a D in reading first term and was placed on academic probation. He would have given up if it if not been for Clarice.

ARE YOU OUT OF YOUR F------G MIND?

Byron's mother was a force of nature. One of seven children raised in a shotgun house in Apex, North Carolina, Clarice was the daughter of a good providing but bad drinking father who sometimes beat his wife and chased his children into the woods. Clarice learned to stay out his way and to work hard. She went to college while making hats for women and laboring in sewing factories. She taught that same obedience and diligence to her children.

Her motto was, "Work hard, pray hard, treat people right, and good things will happen." That formula did not always work for her, for she had two failed marriages. But she still believed in it, and insisted that her three children live it out.

She made sure that Byron worked hard, and didn't have idle time. He was to take advantage of every opportunity to get extra credit, go to school, come home to do work around the house, go to sports practice, then homework, and church whenever the doors were open. No friends at home unless she was there, no parties at the house, only dances sponsored by the school, and church events. No teen hangouts or the mall.

Curfew on Fridays was eleven. When Byron pleaded for more time, Clarice snapped, "Nothing good ever happens after midnight."

She did whatever was necessary to get Byron into good schools, even if it meant begging the principal. She chose Archbishop Curley High School for Byron because he would get a good education there. Besides, it would provide discipline, which was never far from her mind: "They will whoop your ass as quickly as I will if you get out of line."[150]

They didn't have to whoop him, because Clarice kept him in line. After all that discipline and hard work, and the patient laboring over letters and words, he gradually began to enjoy them. He came to love history, and joined the school newspaper as a sports writer. It thrilled him to see people reading his stories. By senior year he was a solid B student, ranking thirtieth out of a class of 240. Four years earlier he had been twenty from the bottom.

Despite the discipline and good education, Byron did poorly in his first term at Ohio Wesleyan College. He was still a very slow reader, and didn't have teachers watching over him as they did in high school. Because of his stuttering, he slipped back into his old silence, which he had partially broken out of in high school. These college classes moved too quickly for him to get beyond the limited range of words he had gradually learned to get out without stuttering. After he got a D+ on an English midterm exam, the professor told him, "Mr. Pitts, you are wasting your time and the government's money. You are not Ohio Wesleyan material. I think you should leave."[151]

Byron despaired. He dropped hints in phone calls to his mother that he might quit.

Soon he received a letter written in red ink. That was the color she used when she was mad. Over the course of his college career Clarice wrote Byron more than 150 letters, but this was her most famous (his friends got a kick out of reading them).

> Dear Mr. Brain Dead,
>
> Have you lost your f-----g mind? You went to Ohio Wesleyan with the express goal of graduating, going on to live your dreams and God's purpose for your life. At the first sign of trouble you want to give up. Fine! Bring your ass back to Baltimore and get a job. Maybe if you think you're up for it, enroll in Bay College. There are plenty of places in the city for dummies. Yep, come home with your tail between your legs and get some half-ass job and spend the rest of your life crying about what you could have been. . . .
>
> You are a gift from God. The Lord I serve does not make mistakes. You did not go to Ohio Wesleyan because you are so smart or worked so hard. You got here because of prayer and faith and God's grace. . . .
>
> Don't get scared or lazy. Don't just cry. Figure out what God is teaching you, then get your ass back [to that school] and keep pulling hard and looking forward.
>
> Son, you know your momma loves you. I believe in you. I pray for you. I know you better than you know

yourself. And I know a God who is able. You're not coming home. You're not going to give up. You're not going to fail. You are going to endure.

Love, Mom

THE ANGEL FROM ESTONIA

Byron appreciated his mother's love, but he thought his English professor was more realistic. That professor knew that Byron didn't have what it takes. He really didn't belong there.

He was on his way to dropping out when along came an angel from Estonia.

Professor Ülle Lewes was a refugee from that war-torn country, driven out after her country was bombed by both the Soviets and the Germans in World War II. Byron's first year at Ohio Wesleyan was also her first year there as a professor, after a short teaching stint at Temple University and a graduate degree in English from Harvard. Perhaps because she too felt like an outsider, she saw and heard what others didn't—a young man weeping on a bench outside University Hall, with a withdrawal slip in his hand.

When Byron told her he was stupid and didn't belong at that college, she told him to stop speaking such nonsense, and to come talk to her the next day in her office. That began three and a half years of mentoring, in which Bryon learned to pay attention to details of language, and how to structure a paper.

She gave Byron her own grades for papers he got back from other professors—some were higher and some lower—and pushed him relentlessly to correct every grammatical mistake. She taught him to make an argument on paper in logical order so that each part led naturally to the next.

It paid off. By the time he graduated, he was one of the school's top graduates in journalism.

But in the meantime, he also came under the tutelage of Dr. Ed Robinson, a speech professor who taught Byron how to compensate for stuttering.

PENCILS IN THE MOUTH

Robinson was gruff and blunt, and had no special training in speech therapy. But he cared, and the work he did with Byron helped transform his speech. Perhaps thinking of Demosthenes's proclaiming with pebbles in his mouth, Robinson had Pitts read out loud with pencils in his mouth. He brought the journalism student down to the college radio station, and made him sit in a booth for thirty minutes at a time, reading Shakespeare or the sports page, backwards and forwards.

Then the professor enrolled Byron in a theater course called "The Actor's Voice," where he learned about breathing from the abdomen, and coordinating breath with speech.

Finally, Professor Robinson made Byron become a host at the radio station. Amazingly, he never stuttered in all his time on the air there, even though his days of stuttering were not over. His secret was to sing his sentences when he got into trouble, remembering how preachers at his church sometimes sang their words in a sermon.

Perhaps the best advice the professor gave Byron was to "keep working and practicing." Never to give up working on the problem, always taking time to plan what he was going to say. "Concentrate! Slow down! Breathe!" he would say over and over.

Those three commands were critical for Pitts as he became a TV journalist. He still had times when he would block, and there were always words and phrases which he avoided. "But the practice of pausing and gathering my thoughts before speaking has served me well as a journalist."[152]

THE SHAME OF SNOW

And what a career he has had! Chief national correspondent for *The CBS Evening News*, contributor to the newsmagazine *60 Minutes*, lead reporter during the September 11 attacks, the Iraq War, Hurricane Katrina, the war in Afghanistan, the refugee crisis in Kosovo, and the Boston bombings.

But long before he started his rise to national fame, he worked for a TV station in Norfolk, Virginia. On a rare morning when it snowed, he was doing a story on corruption in county politics. He had his story down pat, memorized in his head, waiting for the anchor to turn to him. When he did, he asked Pitts a question about the weather.

This was a question Pitts was completely unprepared for. He started saying that it was beginning to snow, but couldn't get past the "s" in snow. After stammering "s-s-s-s-s-snow," the cameraman mercifully turned the camera to snow on the ground, which gave Pitts a moment to think. After the pause, he was able to go into his memorized bit about corruption without a hitch.

That night shame flooded him. He watched the segment over and over again to learn what not to do in the future—namely, panic when caught off guard. Never panic, he told himself, but take a moment to think and then slowly speak. Pitts says he still feels the shame, years later.

THE FOURFOLD SECRET

In the years since, Pitts has still struggled with certain words and phrases, but says he has never stuttered on the air. His secret has been a combination of things he learned from his mother and the hard knocks of life: preparation, paying attention, humor, and faith.

1. *Be prepared.* Pitts says the trick to not stuttering on the air is to carefully prepare and rehearse everything he plans to say. He works out in his mind ahead of time every destination, and the beginning and end of every speech. Not to mention, of course, the content of each speech or report. This is what he calls the blue collar approach—the hard work his mother drilled into him.

The preparation starts at the beginning of every day. "Before my feet hit the floor in the morning, I remember three things about myself: I am a Christian, I am a stutterer, and I am an African-American man. Other people probably think of me as a black man, a stutterer, and maybe a Christian. But knowing who I am helps prepare me for what might happen that day."[153]

Even then, however, it is rarely easy. He had a narrow miss in Boston when he covered the aftermath of the bombing at the Boston Marathon.

> I was outside my comfort zone. We were near Cambridge Ridge High School, in the neighborhood where the two brothers [who have been indicted for the bombings] lived. I found an auto mechanic to interview, to get his reactions. He had very little to say, which left me with a big empty space on air. I started walking up the street, with nothing left to say that I could think of. So I said, "It's chaotic here . . . I'd like you to absorb the moment," and went silent as the camera panned the street filming frenzied policemen securing the area.[154]

In that moment he took the advice he learned in Norfolk—don't panic, but pause and think.

2. *Watch for triggers.* Pitts says he watches himself for the times when he is nervous, scared, angry, or tired. He knows those are warning signals—that he could soon lose control of his tongue. So he takes whatever action is necessary to protect himself against his "demons," by pausing and praying when he is nervous or scared, calming himself when he is angry, and napping when he is tired. He works out regularly to stay fit, for he has learned that when he is out of shape he gets frustrated, and the frustration can lead to loss of self-control.

3. *Humor.* On January 22, 2003, Pitts was in Baghdad covering the American invasion of Iraq. There was a rumor in the air that Saddam Hussein's two sons had been killed in a firefight with American forces in Mosul. Pitts was playing cards in his hotel room with his producer Mike Solmsen when they heard a loud round of gunfire just outside their building. It sounded like the hotel was under attack.

"What should we do?" Pitts asked Solmsen.

"It's pretty obvious. Get under the table, call New York, and finish our hand."

Both Pitts and his producer burst into laughter. It was just what they needed at a time of high tension.[155]

It turned out that the gunfire came from the Arab custom of shooting into the air at a moment of celebration. Saddam's sons were dead indeed.

4. *Faith.* Pitts's life is buoyed by his faith. He says he never makes a major decision without soaking it in prayer first. He adds, he says, his mother's qualification, "Lord, not my will but yours be done."

Pitts says this has been his principal way to cope with the agonies of stuttering. From the time he was a boy, he knew that somehow God had allowed this speech problem for his good. "I have learned that everything is a tool to live a more godly life."[156] And that stuttering was part of his "gifting."

But how could that be? How could stuttering be a gift?

RELATING TO THE UNDERDOG

Pitts learned what many of the subjects in this book learned, that stuttering helped shape his character for the good. In fact, he now believes that the deep pain he suffered as a stutterer—and as someone who felt behind in school for so many years—was a superb preparation for his career as a journalist.

First, it gave him empathy for those who suffer. "I know what it's like to be wounded. I can relate to the underdog, since I have always felt like I was an underdog."[157] Besides, he says, as a journalist it is his job to comfort the afflicted and afflict the comfortable. He can bring comfort to those in pain, especially emotional pain, because he has felt it for much of his life. It helps him create a bond with those who are afflicted.

Second, stuttering has taught him to listen, and that is perfect training for a good journalist. Listening long and hard, especially after asking the right questions, enables a reporter to get at what is most important and telling.

Spending years not being *able* to speak has made Byron Pitts into a world-class journalist now *able* to speak in a singular way.

Chapter 12

America's "last true man of letters": John Updike

Until John Updike (1932–2009), no one had ever described stuttering with such dead-on precision. Once he compared it to a traffic jam. "I have lots of words inside me: but at moments, like rush-hour traffic at the mouth of a tunnel, they jam."[158]

He painted a picture of facial tics that will make any relative of a stutterer groan with recognition.

> Viewing myself on taped television, I see the repulsive symptoms of an approaching stammer take possession of my face—an electronically rapid flutter of the eyelids, a distortion of the mouth as of a leather purse being cinched, a terrified hardening of the upper lip, a fatal tensing and lifting of the voice.[159]

All stutterers will nod knowingly when they hear him refer to that "untrustworthy" part of himself that "can collapse at awkward or anxious moments into a stutter." They might smile at his philosophical conclusion that stuttering is a sign of the "duality of our existence, the ability of the body and soul to say no to one another." Or his reflection that a stammer is the acknowledgement of unacknowledged complexities surrounding even the simplest of verbal exchanges.[160]

They might laugh, as I did, when they read his depiction of stuttering as negotiating an obstacle course with an unhappy ending: "Sometimes, it is as if I have, hurrying to the end of my spoken sentence, carefully picked and plotted my way out of a room full of obstacles, and having almost attained (stealthily, cunningly) the door, I trip, calling painful attention to myself and spilling all the beans."[161]

ADULTEROUS AND RELIGIOUS

Winner of two Pulitzer Prizes and scores of others, Updike is best known for his graphic but lyrical portrayal of the sexual infidelities of middle America in the 1960s and beyond. It was not for nothing that he was called the poet laureate of modern adultery. The most famous of his sixty-odd books was *Couples*, the story of a band of spouse-trading friends, one of whom greeted her lover with the legendary words, "Welcome to the post-pill paradise."[162]

Surprisingly, Updike was stubbornly religious throughout his life. He told an interviewer, "I'm a religious writer . . . I try to show people stuck with this kind of yearning [for other men's wives and for morality and religion]."[163] He was a regular church-goer, recited the Lord's Prayer with his children when he tucked them in for bed at night, and defended Christian theism from his days at Harvard in the early 1950s until his death sixty years later. Even *Couples* is shot through and through with religion. The two principal adulterers are the only regular churchgoers in the book; its fictional town Tarbox (modelled after Updike's real town oh Ipswich, Massachusetts) has streets called Charity and Divinity leading to the Congregational Church with its "pricking steeple and flashing cock"; and the end of the story climaxes with the destruction of the church by lightning, suggesting divine judgment. The main antagonist and adulterer Piet concludes, "God doesn't love us anymore."[164]

Updike was a man of many contradictions. Spiritual *and* religious, he was a serial adulterer. Widely celebrated as one of America's greatest writers, his work was dismissed by some critics as stylized pornography with nothing serious to say. Although he recognized the devastation the sexual revolution was wreaking on families, he abandoned his first wife and children to marry one of his mistresses. Often frustrated by his tongue, he found freedom in the written word to write about sex and love in ways that titillated and enchanted millions of readers. Yet the millions of words he produced caused some to complain that he hid behind them because what mattered more to him than either of those human mysteries was his own need to be heard.

Updike was also a man who stuttered. Although his stutter was mild, and he found his own ways to tame it, the stuttering itself provides us a clue to how he could live with all these contradictions. It was a sign of much of the rest of his life—filled with inner contradictions, he was able to manage them and succeed in many ways. His stutter caused him inner frustration and heartache, but to others it was barely noticeable. He worked hard to keep his unruly tongue under discipline. Sometimes it got out of hand, but he figured ways most of the time to keep it under control. Thus he was able to soldier on, with enormous professional success.

The rest of his life was similar. The contradictions remained. But because of his inner philosophy involving God and sex, he was able to quiet his conscience when it threatened to undo him. He managed to keep the inner contradictions at bay, at a stalemate, so he could get on with what was always most important to him—his writing.

AMERICA'S LAST TRUE MAN OF LETTERS

Updike was one of the most celebrated American writers of the twentieth century. He is the only American to have *twice* won each of the following prestigious literary awards—the Pulitzer Prize, the National Book Award, and the O. Henry Prize.

These prizes were well-deserved. Nearly all the critics, even those who eventually dismissed him, spoke of his phenomenal powers of description. Adam Gopnik of *The New Yorker* said he was the first American writer since Henry James to get the two sides of fiction right, the "precise, realist, encyclopedic appetite to get it all in, and the exquisite urge to make writing out of sensation rendered exactly." Harold Bloom writes of sentences "beyond praise," and James Wood of Updike's ability to write "the perfect sentence." For Updike that perfection always involved the aesthetic, for his aim, he wrote, was "to give the mundane its beautiful due."[165] For example, in *Couples* he looks through the eyes of his protagonist, the builder Piet Hanema, at one of his favorite houses.

> He loved how this house welcomed into itself in every season lemony flecked rhomboids of sun whose slow sliding revolved it with the day, like the cabin of a ship on curving course.[166]

Yet while Updike was best known for his writing about infidelity, his range of subjects and genres was remarkable. His seventeen volumes of short stories prompted Lorrie Moore to call him "American literature's greatest short story writer."[167] His novels include historical fiction (*Memories of the Ford Administration*), magical realism (*Brazil*), science fiction (*Toward the End of Time*), Shakespearean midrash (*Gertrude and Claudius*), historical saga (*In the Beauty of the Lilies*), and political drama (*The Coup*). At the end of his life he was working on a novel about St. Paul and the early church. His most enduring works were written in series—the Rabbit novels about middle-class paragon Rabbit Angstrom, the Bech books about Jewish novelist Henry Bech, and the Maples stories about a troubled marriage (in *Too Far To Go*). His "Scarlet Letter Trilogy" is a modern revision of the Hawthorne classic.

As if all that were not enough, Updike left behind fourteen other volumes of literary criticism, which caused novelist Philip Roth to extol his rival Updike as a writer who was "as brilliant a literary critic and essayist as he was a novelist and short story writer."[168] Little wonder that Charles McGrath gushed that Updike was America's "last true man of letters,"[169] and that just before he died Updike was selected to present the 2008 Jefferson Lecture, the US government's highest humanities honor.

WRITING AS LOVE

For Updike, writing, which he said was his "addiction," was also an act of love. Love for God, who "is the God of the living," not "the God who chastises life and forbids and says No." He learned through his Lutheran Sunday School lessons, even in their "clumsy" attempts to say it, that life is a blessing, and that he was called to accept that blessing. In return for that gift, he was offering "only a nickel a week and my art, my poor little art."[170]

The heart of that art, the heart of true writing, was imitation. To get the world and human relationships right was to imitate properly. If done right, "imitation is praise." So the art of describing accurately, which means to show the beauty of all that is, even in its tragedy, is to express love. Faith in this God of blessing gave Updike courage to tell it like it is. "What small faith I have has given me what artistic courage I have. My theory was that God already knows everything and cannot be shocked."[171]

Even in the grittiness of sexuality there is goodness and beauty, shocking as it is to many. His job was to show it all, especially what has been hidden from view by the worst kinds of tradition. "The world is good, our intuition is, confirming its Creator's appraisal as reported in the first chapter of Genesis." But prudery and bad art have kept us from the goodness and beauty of created life. "Habit and accustomedness have painted over pure gold with a dull paint that can, however, be scratched away, to reveal the shining underbase."[172]

Updike's biographer Adam Begley concludes that Updike saw his writing as a series of "acts of worship." His lyrical descriptions of ordinary human life, lovingly depicted in all of its most shocking detail, expressed love for the Creator. His literary art was a service to God that purified all that was tawdry in the world: "From a higher, inhuman point of view, only truth, however harsh, is holy. The fabricated truth of poetry and fiction makes a shelter in which I feel safe. . . . Such writing is in essence pure. Out of soiled and restless life, I have refined my books. They are trim, crisp, clean . . . before the reviewers leave their smudges all over them."[173]

INCORRIGIBLE GREED AND BAD SEX

Like all great writers, however, Updike had critics who nipped at his heels, suggesting that neither his style nor his substance were as solid as his fame suggested. David Lodge, who otherwise saw religious merit in his work, complained of Updike's "incorrigible greed for stylistic effect." John W. Aldridge sniped that Updike did not possess the attributes of a great literary talent because he lacked "an interesting mind." Harold Bloom, who as we saw praised Updike's style, nevertheless dismissed the Pennsylvania native as a "minor novelist with a major style." Bloom wrote condescendingly that Updike "specializes in easier pleasures." Hovering always near greatness, "the American Sublime will never touch his pages." The UK's *Literary Review* magazine said that even the subject for which his writing is most infamous—sex—is poorly done. In 2008 he was given the Bad Sex in Fiction Lifetime Achievement Award, which celebrates "crude, tasteless or ridiculous sexual passages in modern literature."[174]

I started this last chapter by saying that Updike was a man of contradictions. This is certainly one of them: he was widely regarded for both his style and insight into modern America, yet at the same time he was derided for excessive attention to style and superficial reflection. Even the greatest writers are criticized of course, but this tension or irony is worth noting because it parallels the other contradictions and ironies in his conflicted career, especially those involving morality and religion. Before we turn to his stuttering as another sign of these inner contradictions, let's take a deeper look into his religion, for it is one of the central themes in all of his writing. In fact, his religion connects his near-obsession with sex to his own family conflicts, and helps explain why his family problems exacerbated his stuttering.

SEX AS DIVINE

Begley reports that Updike "threw himself with reckless enthusiasm into the tangle of Ipswich infidelities." Updike conceded in his memoirs that he had slept around in Ipswich, "a stag of sorts in our herd of housewife-does."[175]

How could a man be so religious and yet be so enthusiastic for infidelity? And the very infidelities which he says aggravated his stuttering?

The answer lies in his religion. It was a strange sort of Christianity that rejected the strictures of traditional faith, choosing divine comfort while rejecting divine commands. In other words, it was gospel without law, grace without repentance, the love of God without the holiness of God.

To be sure, Updike held on to parts of historic Christian belief. He rejected philosophical materialism as a failure to make sense of emotion and conscience, and defended Christ's divinity against his first wife's Unitarianism. But at the same time he took from Kierkegaard the idea that Christian faith is subjective in intellectual terms, not a conclusion from rationality or objectivity. So he insisted that resurrection from the dead is "unthinkable" to the modern mind, that God can be known only as "the self projected onto reality" by our natural optimism, and that the closer one moves toward Christianity the more it disappears, "as the fog solidly opaque in the distance thins to transparency when you walk into it."[176]

Updike's Christianity was a religion of self-affirmation. His greatest fears were of death and its threat of nothingness. But religion, he wrote, "enables us to ignore nothingness and get on with the jobs of life." It puts us at ease, reassuring us that our efforts are not futile. So for us in this age of anxiety, God is a "tranquilizer." He reinforces the "endless pardon we bring to our own self." He guarantees the meaning of our existence and serves as "a protector"—even in those moments when he recalled the abortion one of his lovers procured after a tryst with him. Updike's God helped him to, as Begley puts it, "cherish whatever happened to him."[177]

If Updike's God seemed to affirm whatever he did, this included his affairs. For in a manner not unlike that of D. H. Lawrence, Updike viewed sex as a mystical route to the divine. "Sex is the foremost means," he told a CBS interviewer, "of conducting the moral and religious search." It brings "ecstasy" and a sense of "transcendence." Begley reports that it was his adulterous passion that "made him feel alive." He said as much himself: "To give myself brightness and air I [used to] read Karl Barth and fell in love with other men's wives."[178]

So too for his characters in his fiction. When one of the *Couples* adulterers found in his lover a beauty she did not find in herself, he was reminded of his own beauty and the way sex brought down divine power: "This generosity of perception returned upon himself; as he lay with Janet, lost in praise, Harold felt as if a glowing tumor of eternal life were consuming the cells of his mortality." In the novel *A Month of Sundays* a Rev. Marshfield concludes that his first mistress helped reclaim "a wedge of mankind for the Good and the Beautiful," and preaches in a sermon that "the sacrament of marriage . . . exists but as a precondition for the sacrament of adultery." Critic Marshall Boswell opines that Marshfield at this point "about two-thirds believes [this], and Updike about half." Rev. Marshfield rationalizes the seduction of his divinity professor's daughter by proclaiming, "I was slaying him that the Lord might live." Kathleen Verduin observes that for Updike illicit sex can become "an act of righteous punishment."[179]

A RATHER ANTINOMIAN CHRISTIANITY

In Updike's religion, then, there are no commandments we are meant to keep except the obligation to accept what is: "Religion includes, as its enemies say, fatalism, an acceptance and consecration of what is." Our only responsibility is to "appreciate" the great gift that life represents. He learned from Barth that the next life is simply this life in review, and from his Lutheranism, he wrote, "a rather antinomian Christianity"—the idea that there are no laws we should fear or live by—which he was "too timid to discard." There is no hint of final judgment. Nor is there any imperative to repent or improve ourselves: in Begley's words, "Original sin may be inescapable, but any concerted effort to improve one's game resembles a righteous struggle for salvation." And if there was anything he learned from Barth, it was that all human efforts to save ourselves are wrongheaded and futile. As one critic summed it up, Updike "radically divorced" Christian theology from Christian ethics.[180]

The upshot was a self-indulgent religion that basked in self-affirmation while running from voices that would challenge the self to change, particularly in ways that are not pleasant. It is telling that Updike's last poem ends with words of self-assurance from Psalm 23: "goodness and mercy shall follow me all / the days of my life, my life, forever."[181]

STUTTERING AND GUILT

Perhaps not surprisingly, this sensual religion justified the family conflicts which exacerbated Updike's stuttering. The religion encouraged him to seek his own authenticity, even if it meant cheating on his wife. The result was a new feeling of self-worth, but also new problems with his speech. "With my own children, after I left them [and his first wife Mary], I developed a sharp and painful stutter that had not been there before." When he moved out of the family house to take up residence on his own, he began to stutter with his own children. "Stuttering had not been a problem for years. Suddenly I was afraid, again, of being misunderstood, of being mistaken for somebody else. I doubted my worthiness to mar the air with my voice."[182]

Updike knew that his stuttering was caused by faulty breathing ("we arrive at our ridiculous spasm when in truth we are out of breath, when in our haste and anxiety we have forgotten to breathe"), and thought that getting out of his first marriage would help. But when he tried to break out, he had "trouble breathing." Later, he said, the marriage was squeezing his chest. Eventually it left him feeling "breathlessness" and "panic." Yet, in another one of the many contradictions of his life, getting free from the marriage brought on a new kind of stuttering, a new trouble with breathing.[183]

In this case Updike's stuttering was connected to guilt. He didn't know why he could not choose between Mary and his mistress, and felt guilty about being caught in the middle. He felt guilty about being too busy to delight in his children, except when they were asleep. He was too busy "falling in love, away from marriage," as he put it. He even felt guilty about not feeling guilty enough, reproaching himself for being "rapacious, sneaky, and remorseless." He knew that his adulteries were hurting his children. As a character in *Couples* observed, "What we give [our children] is neglect so subtle they don't even notice it."[184]

There were times when the contradictions within his religion poked above the surface. When Richard Maples offers to bow his head at night to pray with his daughter and she cries softly, "Daddy, no, don't!" Begley suggests this is Updike's recognition that piety can be false, belied by parents who by their infidelities neglect their children. Even after he married his mistress Martha, his children felt deprived. Martha rationed his time with his kids, so that his son Michael complained, "It felt like we're his mistress and he's sneaking away from Martha to see us." Updike was experiencing such moral confusion that he started seeing a psychiatrist every other week.[185]

But the guilt was not enough to make him stop. Though he recognized the danger of "monstrous self-absorption" in Ipswich, Begley says he yielded to it: "Distracted by work, by his gang of friends, by his many flings, Updike was only fitfully aware of his children's problems." Even in his older years after he had moved with Martha out of Ipswich, he let Martha screen out the kids whenever she judged it necessary to protect his time to write. Another son, David, told a BBC reporter that his father had decided early on that his writing would "take precedence over his relations with real people." On his deathbed at a hospice, when Mary and the children asked for more time with John, Martha told them it would not be possible.[186]

Dear reader, I am not suggesting that guilt caused Updike's stuttering, or that inner psychology is the root cause of any stuttering, in the vast majority of cases. But there is no doubt that emotional tension makes stuttering worse, and sometimes causes stuttering that has for a time remained dormant, to suddenly flare up again. It is clear in Updike's case that his later flare-ups of stuttering were connected to his guilt over the problems he was causing his family, which were supported by the strange religious brew he had concocted over the years.

So his religion, sexual obsessions, and speech problems were all connected. He was able to keep cheating on his wives and lovers despite the pain he knew he was causing his family because he kept telling himself that his sexual liaisons were ways to make him feel good about himself and connect to God. This is how he was able to live with the guilt, and convince himself that in the end he would not be condemned. Similarly, the new troubles with stuttering which his unfaithfulness prompted could be endured because that unfaithfulness helped him stave off fear of death and nothingness. Stuttering, then, was the sign of all those earthly woes that are necessary on the pilgrimage to divine ends. Like guilt and perhaps even his God, it could be managed so as not to intrude unduly on his preferred life.

WAYS TO COPE

But in the meantime, how *did* Updike manage his stuttering? He never conquered it with the finality we saw in John Stossel. Nor did he continually struggle to the degree that Annie Glenn does. Updike's stammer was mild, barely perceptible. People who are not familiar with stuttering might even be unaware that it was there, or that it was a continual source of strain and frustration to a razor-sharp mind like Updike's, especially to one who has so many words to speak in such exquisite ways. He said, for example, that he feared speaking before audiences, especially New York audiences. He knew that he stuttered more when he thought he was in the wrong, which is how he felt when he was with policemen, Israeli journalists and intellectuals, his children, and generally with men. He felt more at ease with women, people from his hometowns, literary people, and people who wanted something from him. He tended to stutter when he was defending something unpopular, such as the Vietnam War in the late 1960s and early 70s. He still felt shame when his speech would lapse.[187]

But he learned to be wary of triggers—such as being tired and drinking too much. He discovered that getting angry could actually help him speak more fluently. Most important, he had seen that breathing is critical, so that he must remember to take a breath and make sure he did not keep speaking after he had run out of air. Therefore it helped to speak more slowly.[188]

But most comforting was his delight in writing. He often felt his speech was "halting," even if his hearers did not pick up on that. But he received near-infinite pleasure from being able to express his thoughts "smoothly," with all the precise beauty and diction that he could muster.[189]

NOT ENTIRELY UNFORTUNATE

Like most of our famous stutterers, Updike never wished for a life without stuttering. He said it was "not entirely unfortunate" that he was saddled with this affliction. He noticed that those who spoke too easily caused their listeners to distrust them, suspecting that their words must hide some sort of deception. The stutterer, on the other hand, "wins," because in his pauses he elicits "respectful attention" and "tender alertness" in his auditors. They sense that the stutterer must have an "excess of sensibility" or feeling. The person who has suffered with such an ever-present and humiliating handicap must know what it is like for others to suffer, at least to some degree. Heart speaks to heart, and the mere sound of frustration communicates a kind of empathy.[190]

Despite Updike's evident flaws, he had one virtue that could be of great help to other stutterers. For that matter, to all of us, speech defect or no. Through his whole life he was buoyed by an underlying joy for life. Mere human experience was always a sense of wonder and delight for him. In his memoir he wrote, "Reality is gratuitous," which for him meant life as a free gift we do not deserve. He might have said that we could have been created as cockroaches but instead found ourselves thrown onto this globe as seeing and hearing and tasting human beings, with all the pleasures those sensations bring. Life is about ever-new views of things, and "in truth all views have something glorious about them. The act of seeing is itself glorious, and of hearing, and feeling, and tasting." He praised one of his golf partners who remarked once, "Life is bliss," and then on another fairway, "Ah, to be alive, on a June day, in Ipswich, Massachusetts!"[191]

The point, according to Updike, was that the key to happiness is not having certain things happen to us, but to recognize that there is a basic underlying happiness beyond any particular cause for it. Just to be alive is a gift. Other novelists highlighted the tragedies of life, and suggested that life might not be worth living. Not John Updike. For this novelist at the end of the twentieth century, the bloodiest of all centuries, the point was to tap into the mystery of existence itself, and to find the beauty in the ordinary. That is what he spent his life trying to do. Even if we might not agree with his religion or his morality, we might learn from this glass-half-full approach, which saw beauty everywhere. That is something that can help everyone, not just stutterers.

Twelve lessons for stutterers
(and the rest of us)

What can we learn from these twelve inspiring stories?

Plenty. Not only about stuttering, but about life more generally.

These are lessons that will help stutterers cope with their own affliction. They might help some take steps toward overcoming—either by getting beyond a particular roadblock or moving dramatically toward a very different lifestyle. They might be motivated, as I was, to undertake intensive stuttering therapy that changes their lives. Or they might devise their own creative ways, as Joshua Chamberlain did, to speak in public while keeping their stuttering in check.

But these lessons are not just for stutterers. They can help all of us deal with the addiction or handicap that besets us. And who does not have such a problem? Most or all of us discover after a few years of life that we too have an affliction that would prevent us from reaching our goals if we let it. These lessons can help us make sure that *our* personal demon does not control our life.

1. *It's not the end of the world.*

Yes, stuttering is a pain. It makes us feel angry, discouraged, and frustrated. But there are worse things. Think of Stephen Hawking, the brilliant physicist who is not only paralyzed by ALS (Lou Gehrig's disease) but cannot speak. He communicates by using a small sensor that is activated by a muscle in his cheek. He uses this sensor to "type" characters and numbers on his keyboard. It's an old platitude, but worth remembering nonetheless: "Remember those who are worse off than you." It helps us to recall that stuttering does not mean our lives are ruined.

There is also the danger of self-obsession. I remember complaining in college to an older friend about how stuttering frustrated me. He spoke gently but I felt the rebuke. "Gerry, are you going to let this obsess you? There is more to life than this." He was telling me that if I chose to focus on this to the exclusion of everything else, I was missing out on the joys of life. And that I was letting myself become self-absorbed.

Moses was forced out of his self-pity by the voice in the biblical story. As a result, he discovered that stuttering did not cripple him. He still stuttered, but he managed to lead a nation through perilous times.

Annie Glenn told herself, in the long years before she got life-changing help, that there was more to life than her speech. If she could not get her words out on a given day, so what? She found ways to be happy regardless. She still reached out to friends, and found joy by using her gift of music.

2. *Stuttering need not prevent great success.*

Every one of the twelve famous stutterers in this book achieved great success. Their stories show that our stuttering, while an obstacle, need not prevent us from reaching our goals. We might not become great speakers, but we can be successful in life even with this struggle.

Of course, some stutterers become excellent speakers anyway. Winston Churchill and John Stossel are remarkable illustrations of that. They found, one on his own and the other through excellent therapy, ways to speak with power, even though neither found complete freedom from stuttering.

Aristotle might have struggled more than Churchill and Stossel. He wrote with precision about the agonies of stuttering—such accuracy that suggests personal experience. Yet Aristotle accomplished great things. He is widely regarded as one of the greatest thinkers, perhaps the greatest, of the ancient world.

You and I will probably never achieve that kind of greatness. But we can learn from Aristotle and these famous stutterers that our speech problem need not keep us from doing great things.

3. Perseverance and self-discipline are powerful tools.

Demosthenes was probably not a stutterer, but he had real speech problems, as I argued in chapter 3. He had a weak voice, and could not pronounce correctly words that started with "r." Yet Demosthenes became a great orator, known for his powerful speaking, by dogged determination. He worked and worked and worked to overcome these speech difficulties. He practiced his speeches in a cave, repeated words with the "r" sound thousands of times, and ran up hills to strengthen his weak frame. Greater body strength helped him project his voice, which was essential in a world without microphones.

Chamberlain, as we saw, labored ceaselessly to overcome his speech problem. He resolved when he was young that this problem was "intolerable." He would stand for it no longer. Rather than despair, he determined he would do whatever it took to find improvement. By strength of will and using a songlike rhythm, he eventually reached a state where he could get through nine out of of ten difficult words with no trouble.

That ratio might stop ordinary persons from ever speaking in public again. But for Chamberlain, it was a great improvement. He went on to serve successfully as governor, college president, and lecturer on the speaking circuit.

The lesson? Don't give up. Even if your plight seems hopeless, it is probably not. Many other stutterers have been in your situation, and many have found ways to cope, carry on, and make improvements. Some, like Chamberlain, have succeeded in heroic fashion. So take heart! Get some help from a therapist who has a proven track record with stutterers. Take the advice you are given by the therapist, and practice, practice, practice. Things will change, most likely for the better.

4. Look for your own creative ways to get better.

Chamberlain found his own creative way. He attacked his three troublesome sounds by learning to "skip lightly over" them, using good breath, and then "turning on the will." By the last phrase he meant always using this method, and not giving up just because he had trouble from time to time.

Other characters in this book developed their own methods. Each one was somewhat unique, fitted for his or her particular situation. The "breathy voice" seemed to work, at least much of the time, for Marilyn Monroe.

John Stossel found his secret from his Hollins therapy, but not until he had already found his own niche in TV news. It was perfect for a stutterer. Rather than being a typical TV reporter who would have to sometimes shout out questions in a tense situation, Stossel chose to do background stories where he could do most of his work far from cameras and at his own pace. It turned out that these stories were deeper and more interesting than the usual weather, catastrophes, and politics in the nightly news. They charted the gradual changes that affected real life more, in areas such as science, economics, ecology, and religion.

Stossel found this niche because he went looking for something that could accommodate his slower speech technique. His success should encourage you to find your own. Be open to what is new and different, and what others have not done.

5. Use stuttering to your advantage.

You're right. Stuttering sucks. It's no one's idea of fun.

But complaining and whining about it won't do a bit of good. Instead, make lemonade out of your lemons. Use your stuttering to your advantage.

That's what King George VI did. He had always listened more than he spoke, because the first was far easier for a stutterer. It turned out that people loved it. Nearly all people want others to listen to them, especially if they feel they have something important to say. When the king was helping lead the nation during the

War, he toured the country and simply listened to people. That showed his respect for them and all that they were suffering. They loved him for it, and as word got out, he became a people's favorite. He was known for his empathetic listening. People knew that he suffered, and they sensed that he understood what it was to suffer, even if he *was* the king, whose lifestyle seemed to shield him from suffering. For they had heard and read of the pain "stammering" had caused him.

Think of how you can use stuttering to your advantage. Have you ever noticed that intelligent people being interviewed in the media often speak slowly? Remember that when you are tempted to break all the rules and try to speak too quickly. You might find that you are thought to be more intelligent because you choose your words more slowly and deliberately.

Or, when you have to decide between joining a small group chattering about nothing in particular, which always causes you anxiety because of the difficulties of speaking spontaneously, try grabbing the newspaper or a book, and use the time more productively.

Let your stuttering profit you.

6. *Let stuttering do the work in you which it has done in others— deepening their character.*

You have heard it before, and perhaps you thought it a cop-out: that stuttering can help you become a better person.

But it's not a cop out. It is a real thing, if you let it be. That is, if you learn from the lives of the famous stutterers in this book, and let what starts in you develop more fully.

For example, Moses seems to have learned humility from his stuttering. The Bible says he was the most humble man on the earth at that time.[192] We don't know for sure what that means, but no doubt it included his recognizing that he was not perfect, and that he needed help from others. Which, as we saw for King George VI, involved listening to others and thereby showing them that they were worth listening to.

So if your stuttering has helped you to listen to people, consider that the beginning of a virtue, and let it develop. Listen even more. Fix your eyes on the speaker's face; give her your full attention. That practice, if you let it become a habit, will make you a better person.

No doubt your suffering this malady has caused you suffering. Let that knowledge of your own pain cause you to try to feel the pain of others, and express to them your consolation. They will appreciate it. That too will make you a deeper person.

Learn from Peter Brown, whose years of struggling as a student trying to speak has caused him as a professor to keep an eye out for shy students who seem to be struggling. Brown seeks them out, and tries to lend a listening ear and caring heart.

Or perhaps you have learned that after having a bad day with your speech, you were able to get up the next morning and try again. And maybe it went better that next day. Maybe you learned a bit of courage from that—that you need not retreat into silence for the rest of your life, but can come back the next day with a new approach.

That's called courage. You did not let little defeats defeat you.

Take that courage that you have learned from stuttering and apply it to other areas of life. If you have learned to endure the taunts or snickers of others, use that learning to speak up for unpopular people or causes. That is another kind of courage. You will find that if you can be courageous in speaking, you can be courageous in other ways too. Both experiences will show you that it feels good to know you have been courageous. And both will make you a better person.

7. Ponder the benefits stuttering has brought you.

After a bad day stuttering, it can be easy to sink into self-hatred and despair, thinking that things will never get better. It can also be easy to nurse feelings of anger and bitterness, wondering why life has treated you this way when so many of your friends seem to be free of major maladies.

Those are the days when it is good to reflect that no one escapes major problems. If they live too short a life to experience deep affliction, then an early death is itself a serious affliction.

But those are also the days when we need to recall the benefits which stuttering has brought you. Otherwise we will be destroyed emotionally by bitterness and self-pity.

John Stossel reflects in just this way. He realizes that stuttering led him, without his realizing it at the time, into a magnificent career. It was precisely because he knew he could not do what major news reporters do—shout out questions with split-second timing—that he threw himself into deep research on stories about slow-moving things. These were better suited to his speech struggle, and were also more interesting to more people. The rest is history.

Being away from the stories that attracted the most reporters also gave him more freedom. Like Einstein, he was more original in his thinking because he was outside of the centers of his discipline. He was freer from the groupthink that plagues every discipline. The result was more creativity.

The same thing was true for Lionel Logue. In Australia, he was thousands of miles away from speech therapy institutes. But that isolation enabled him to think for himself, and develop methods for helping shell-shocked veterans of World War I. It was those methods that he used with considerable success on King George VI.

When John Stossel remembers how the very thing he once lamented proved to be a boon, it frees him from self-pity. He realizes that in this and other ways, stuttering has brought benefits.

Byron Pitts thinks similarly. He says his stuttering has been "a gift." It helped shape his character for the better, and gave him empathy for other sufferers. This helped him create a bond with the afflicted in his new stories, and taught him to listen.

Try to recall the benefits the next time you are in the pit, thinking you will never get out, and maybe even wishing you were never born. It will help restore your hope.

8. Don't take yourself so seriously—learn to laugh.

Remember the friend who in college told me that I was in danger of being obsessed with my stuttering? His point was not to take myself so seriously. I would expound on that by encouraging you to use a little humor.

Marilyn Monroe did just that. As we saw, she suffered painfully from stuttering—as well as battling a host of other demons in her life. But she returned frequently to a wry sense of humor that enabled her to rise above, if only momentarily, the everyday pains.

So did Byron Pitts. When lying under a table in Baghdad during what seemed to be a rocket attack, he and his producer joked and played cards. When Joshua Chamberlain was hit by a bullet that tore through his pelvis, he quipped, "What will my mother say—her boy shot in the back?" Churchill is legendary for his humor, especially during World War II when the whole nation needed a lift. Churchill's wit provided it time and time again.

When Peter Brown hits a snag during a lecture, he jokes to cut the tension.

Laughter is good for the soul. It helps us realize the ironies of life, and can cure us of self-importance.

Norman Cousins (1915–90) was a political journalist who suffered acute pain from a special arthritic condition. He discovered that laughter was medicinal by watching Marx Brothers movies. "I made the joyous discovery that ten minutes of genuine belly laughter had an anesthetic effect and would give me at least two hours of pain-free sleep. When the pain-killing effect of the laughter wore off, we would switch on the motion picture projector again and not infrequently, it would lead to another pain-free interval."[193]

Thousands of years ago a wise man wrote, "A cheerful heart is medicine."[194] It will not cure your stuttering, but it will make it easier to cope.

9. Have you tried writing?

Peter Brown found that writing helped him both to release pent-up emotion and to bring a kind of healing. He did not put it in so many words, but I think he meant that we stutterers get a certain sense of satisfaction by being able to use just the right words in writing—the ones we *really* wanted to say but couldn't—rather than substituting words in order to get to the end of a sentence orally. Finally, I sometimes have thought, *now* I can put in writing, with far more precision and elegance, what I tried to say orally but had to replace with words that were vague and awkward.

Brown told me that writing was also therapeutic for him. It brought a kind of healing. I think he meant that putting things down in writing, in exactly the way he first intended, helped assuage the frustration he felt sometimes in oral lectures. I have felt the same. I tend to labor over what I write, rewriting and rephrasing to get it just right, but gaining a good deal of satisfaction from thinking that now I have gotten my thoughts down in decent form. Of course, some of my readers might think I should have labored more! Or that what I think is good is actually far from it.

You might not be a writer. The thought of writing might conjure up bad memories of high school or college English classes that you hated. You might even prefer getting your teeth drilled without novocaine to writing something formal to be read by others.

But I am not suggesting anything formal. Nor do I think you have to show it to others. Try a personal journal that no one reads but you. Of course at some point you might want to show it to someone else. The purpose is to give yourself a way to express your thoughts without the frustration of speaking. That can provide not only mental relief but a modicum of emotional satisfaction. It could also be a way to communicate with people with a clarity that you could not achieve orally.

This doesn't mean that you give up trying to improve your speech. But while you are on the way toward that goal, you can use writing for both these purposes.

10. Don't let stuttering define you.

Annie Glenn was able to be happy for many years before she got relief from a severe stutter. Trying to shop at an unfamiliar store was torture, but she did not let that ruin her life. She was regularly stymied in ordinary conversation, but found happiness in her music and friendships. Life was still good for her, even though parts of her life were very, very difficult.

In other words, Annie did not let stuttering define her. She did not let stuttering become her identity. She was far more than "a person with a bad stutter." Sure, that was something she was known for. But she decided it was only a small part of who she was. Because that was her attitude, and she did not let stuttering keep her from doing things, people who knew her realized that she was an extraordinary person who was *also* a stutterer.

John Updike also struggled. At times, speaking was torture for him too. But he reveled in life. He accepted his stuttering as one small part of who he was. Of course, you could say there is no wonder he could transcend his stuttering because he was such a great writer—and you have no such extraordinary skills. But there have been plenty of other successful writers who have been miserable, and even taken or tried to take their own lives: Jack London, Kurt Vonnegut, Sylvia Plath, Edgar Allen Poe, Virginia Woolf, Hunter Thompson. Professional success is no guarantee of happiness.

Something more than professional success is needed by everyone, Updike included. He achieved what Annie Glenn found— because he chose to take a positive attitude to life, with its mix of bad and good. Updike chose to believe that life is a gift. He found beauty in the ordinary. He was one of those people who call the glass half-full rather than half-empty. Annie Glenn did the same. Because of choosing that approach to life, neither Updike nor Glenn let stuttering define them.

11. Some tips on mechanics.

There are things we stutterers can do to minimize our slipups. Some of the characters in this book found the following admonitions were helpful:

a. *Don't forget to breathe.* Updike observed that he often forgot to breathe *enough*, and would keep talking after he had run out of breath. I have noticed the same, and discovered in my own therapy at the Hollins Institute that I needed to learn to take full breaths throughout my speech. It helps me to remember that Marilyn Monroe was able to succeed as an actress only because she learned to speak in her famous "breathy" voice— after her time with a speech therapist in Hollywood.

b. *Slow down.* Most of us stutterers speak far too quickly. Getting through difficult words and situations is easier when we slow down. We can concentrate better on what we are doing, and avoid our bad habits. We can more easily plan what to say and how to say it. This was another part of Monroe's success. Not only did she use a breathy voice, but she also tended to speak more slowly than most. Both Byron Pitts and John Updike found that they had fewer problems as speakers when they forced themselves to speak slowly.

c. *Pay attention to triggers.* Two of our famous stutterers found great help by watching for things in their daily patterns that would exacerbate stuttering. One was *nervousness.* Pitts told me that he would adopt special strategies when he knew he was nervous and was about to speak. At those times he shot up a prayer, and tried in his own way to calm himself. I used to dismiss such advice as ridiculous. It made me furious when people said, "Just relax." When I was in a panic, I found it *impossible* to relax. But I have now learned to recognize when my nerves are taut or my heart racing, and to self-consciously slow down and use gentle onsets as I try to slide into sounds that give me trouble.

For both Pitts and Updike, another trigger is *tiredness.* They have noticed that they have more trouble when they were not rested. Pitts adds that being *out of shape* is another trigger, so he tries to work out regularly.

Finally, Updike warned himself to watch out for *drinking too much.* Being slightly intoxicated can make it much more difficult to concentrate on speaking fluently.

I am not suggesting that these tips on mechanics will cure stuttering. I am not so naïve. It took three weeks of twelve-hours-per-day therapy to make a big difference in my speech. I recommend that stutterers get therapy, if they can, from professionals who have a good track record of bringing *significant* improvement to stutterers.

12. Be open to transcendence.

Peter Brown suggests that there is something about stuttering that makes the afflicted wonder if there is more to life than atoms and molecules. Knowing there are ideas to be expressed in beautiful ways and not being able to express them might help stutterers realize their finitude more quickly.

Now of course it is one thing to see that we are finite, and another thing to believe in the infinite. But Brown suggests, and sometimes I agree, that regularly bumping our noses up against walls that limit us can make us wonder if there is a realm where limits do not apply.

On the other hand, stuttering is just one of many maladies in life. There probably is nothing special in our experience of disfluency that makes us more open to transcendence than others. So what Brown suggests is most likely something that happens to millions of people with other maladies that regularly bring frustration.

And we know there are plenty of stutterers who do not think there is another realm that transcends the one known to science. And that some of them have gotten considerable help with their speech nonetheless.

But there are many others like Byron Pitts, who says he could not have made it through his stuttering or life without prayer. He says that God has helped him, and that prayer was his way of connecting.

It is worth considering.

Endnotes

1. The conversations in this chapter are my paraphrases of the words in the Bible in Exodus chapters 2–4.

2. Exodus 4:10.

3. Samuel Davidkin, "The Stuttering Servant," *Jewish Ideas Daily*, 12 April 2012, http://www.jewishideasdaily.com/1109/features/the-stuttering-servant/.

4. Fidias E. Leon-Sarmiento, Edwin Paez, Mark Hallett, "Nature and nurture in stuttering: a systematic review on the case of Moses," *Neurological Science* (2013) 34:231–37.

5. Thanks to Judith Kuster for the notion of choral speaking.

6. Ibid., 235–36.

7. Exodus 2:17. Unless otherwise noted, all translations or paraphrases of the Bible are my own.

8. Diogenes Laertius, *Lives of Eminent Philosophers*, trans. R. D. Hicks, 2 vols. (Cambridge: Harvard University Press, 1972; orig. 1925), 1:445.

9. Aristotle, *Problems*, trans. W. S. Hett (Cambridge: Harvard University Press, 2000; orig. 1936), 228–29, 274–75, 278–81, 288–89, 292–95.

10. Ibid, 292–93.

11. Ibid., 280–81.

12. Ibid., 288–89;

13. Aristotle, *De Audibilis* 804b, in W.D. Ross, *The Works of Aristotle*, vol. VI (Oxford: Clarendon, 1967, orig. 1913). Some think Strato is the real author of this short series of notes (thirteen pages), but it has been included

nonetheless in Aristotle's works.

14. Diogenes Laertius, *Lives of Eminent Philosophers*, 1:445.

15. Henry George Liddell and Robert Scott, *A Greek-English Lexicon* (Oxford: Clarendon, 1996).

16. P. G. W. Glare, *Oxford Latin Dictionary*, 2nd ed. (Oxford: Oxford University Press, 2012).

17. Jonathan Barnes, "Life and Work," in Barnes, ed., *The Cambridge Companion to Aristotle* (Cambridge: Cambridge University Press, 1995), 3–6.

18. That *traulos* was not universally defined as lisping is supported by Hippocrates's (460–370 BCE) use of it in his *Aphorisms* (6.32), where it seems to mean "speech impediment in general," and by Herodotus (484–425 BCE), who used *traulos* to suggest stammering (*The Histories*, 4.155).

19. Benson Bobrick, *Knotted Tongues: Stuttering in History and the Quest for a Cure* (New York: Simon and Schuster, 1995), 64.

20. All the quotations from Plutarch are taken from his chapter on Demosthenes in *Plutarch's Lives*, vol. II, ed. Arthur Hugh Clough (New York: Modern Library, 2001), 387–407.

21. Harvey Yunis, ed., *Demosthenes: On the Crown* (Cambridge: Cambridge University Press, 2001), 211n180.

22. Plutarch, *Plutarch's Lives*, 394.

23. Joshua L. Chamberlain, letter to his wife Fannie, in Thomas Desjardin, ed., *Joshua Chamberlain: A Life in Letters* (Harrisburg, PA: National Civil War Museum, 2012), 172.

24. Historian of the Fifth Corps, quoted in Alice Rains Trulock, *In the Hands of Providence: Joshua L. Chamberlain and the American Civil War* (Chapel Hill: University of North Carolina Press, 1992), 155.

25. James McPherson, "Foreword," in Desjardin, ed., *Joshua Chamberlain: A Life in Letters*, iii.

26. Trulock, *In the Hands of Providence*, 305.

27. Desjardin, ed ., *A Life in Letters*, 228.

28. John J. Pullen, *Joshua Chamberlain: A Hero's Life and Legacy* (Mechanicsburg, PA: Stackpole Books, 1999), 14–16, 111–12; Trulock, *In the Hands of Providence*, 209–19, 316–17, 340, 376, 465–66, 512–13.

29. *"Blessed Boyhood": The 'Early Memoir' of Joshua Lawrence Chamberlain,* eds. Thomas A. Desjardin and David K. Thomson (Brunswick, ME: Bowdoin College Press, 2013), 57–58. The quotations on the next few pages that describe his struggle to master speaking are taken from this memoir, 57–59.

30. Ibid., 67–68.

31. Trulock, *In the Hands of Providence,* 52.

32. *"Blessed Boyhood,"* 59.

33. Edwards G. Longacre, *The Soldier and the Man* (Conshohocken, PA: Combined Publishing, 1999), 21; Desjardin, ed., *A Life in Letters,* 10.

34. Trulock, *In the Hands of Providence,* 120–23; Willard Wallace, *Soul of the Lion: A Biography of Joshua L. Chamberlain* (Gettysburg, PA: Stan Clark Military Books, 1991), 75–76. Michael Shaara's historical novel (*The Killer Angels: A Novel* [New York: David McKay, 1974]) refers to this march, 18. *Killer Angels* received the Pulitzer Prize.

35. Trulock, *In the Hands of Providence,* 147.

36. Ibid., 358.

37. Ibid.

38. Pullen, *Joshua Chamberlain,* 15.

39. Letter quoted in Trulock, *In the Hands of Providence,* 225

40. Letter to Fannie, Jan. 20, 1864, in *Joshua Chamberlain: A Life in Letters,* 223.

41. Edwards G. Longacre: *The Soldier and the Man* (Conshohocken, PA: Combined Publishing, 1999), 292. On his recollections of battle events, see 89–99, 139–40, 200–21; on his marriage, see 261–68, 293; on Catholics and ex-slaves, see 75–76, 251–52, 264, 277, 293.

42. *"Blessed Boyhood!"* 59.

43. *Time,* May 16, 1938.

44. Quoted in Denis Judd, *George VI* (London: I. B. Taurus, 2012), 6.

45. Quoted in Sarah Bradford, *The Reluctant King: The Life and Reign of George VI 1895–1952* (New York: St. Martin's, 1989), 57.

46. Ibid., 119.

47. Judd, *George VI,* 100.

48. Bradford, *The Reluctant King,* 121.

49. Ibid., 122.

50. Mark Logue and Peter Conradi, *The King's Speech: How One Man Saved the British Monarchy* (New York: Sterling, 2010), 71.

51. Bradford, *The Reluctant King,* 124.

52. Ibid., 124.

53. Ibid., 125.

54. Logue and Conradi, *The King's Speech,* 83.

55. Ibid., 85.

56. Judd, *George VI,* 140.

57. Ibid., 140, 143.

58. Logue and Conradi, *The King's Speech,* 125.

59. Bradford, *The Reluctant King,* 212.

60. Logue and Conradi, *The King's Speech,* 131.

61. Ibid., 134.

62. Bradford, *The Reluctant King,* 305.

63. Ibid., 304–5.

64. Ibid., 317.

65. Ibid.

66. Ibid., 325.

67. Logue and Conradi, *The King's Speech,* 185.

68. Ibid., 154.

69. Ibid., 184–85.

70. Ibid., 200.

71. Bradford, *The Reluctant King*, 368.

72. Judd, *George VI*, xv.

73. Logue and Conradi, *The King's Speech*, 229.

74. Ibid.

75. William Manchester, *The Last Lion: Visions of Glory 1874–1932* (Boston: Little, Brown and Co., 1983), 33.

76. Ibid., 29. Of course, he did attend Sandhurst, which is Britain's equivalent to West Point; but Churchill lamented never getting a systematic exposure to the classics. He made up for it by being an autodidact, reading many of them for himself.

77. Randolph S. Churchill, *Winston S. Churchill*, vol. 1, *Youth: 1874–1900* (Boston: Houghton Mifflin, 1966), 282.

78. John Mather, http://www.winstonchurchill.org/learn/myths/myths/he-stuttered.

79. Ibid.

80. William Manchester and Paul Reid, *The Last Lion: Defender of the Realm 1940–1965* (Boston: Boston: Little, Brown and Co., 2012), 3, emphasis added.

81. Manchester, *The Last Lion: Visions of Glory*, 155, emphasis added.

82. William Manchester, *The Last Lion: Alone 1932–1940* (Boston: Little, Brown and Co., 1988), 8.

83. Louis Adamic, *Dinner at the White House* (New York: Harper and Bros, 1946), 30, 32.

84. Louis J. Alber, "When Churchill Lectured in the USA," *American Mercury* (August 1972), 174.

85. Australian Department on Foreign Affairs, *Current Notes on International Affairs* (1937), 249.

86. James Gerard, *My First Eighty-Three Years in America* (New York: Doubleday, 1951), 120.

87. Baron Charles McMoran, *Churchill: Taken from the Diaries of Lord Moran: The Struggle for Survival, 1940–1965* (Dunwoody, GA: Norman S. Berg, 1976), 660, 830.

88. Hans-Peter Schwarz, *Konrad Adenauer: From the German Empire to the Federal Republic, 1876–1952* (New York: Berghahn Books, 1986), 640.

89. Paul Johnson, *Churchill* (New York: Viking, 2009), 2.

90. Mather, http://www.winstonchurchill.org/learn/myths/myths/he-stuttered.

91. Manchester, *The Last Lion: Visions of Glory,* 34.

92. Ibid.

93. Manchester, *The Last Lion: Alone 1932–1940,* 109.

94. Manchester, *The Last Lion: Visions of Glory,* 34.

95. Violet Bonham Carter, *Winston Churchill: An Intimate Portrait* (New York: Harcourt, Brace & World, 1965), 6.

96. Cita Stelzer, *Dinner with Churchill: Policy-Making at the Dinner Table* (New York: Pegasus, 2012), 17, 19.

97. Roy Jenkins, *Churchill: A Biography* (New York: Farrar, Straus and Giroux, 2001), 611.

98. Ibid., 612.

99. John F. Burns, "Seventy Years Later, Churchill's 'Finest Hour' Yields Insights," *New York Times* (June 17, 2010); this "Finest Hour" speech can be found at http://www.fordham.edu/halsall/mod/1940churchill-finest.html.

100. Bonham Carter, *Winston Churchill,* 3–4; emphasis added.

101. Manchester, *The Last Lion: Visions of Glory,* 31.

102. Ibid., 32.

103. Martin Gilbert, *Churchill: A Life* (New York: Henry Holt, 1991), 23.

104. Manchester, *The Last Lion: Visions of Glory,* 35.

105. "I just stuttered," 1960 interview, http://www.youtube.com/watch?v=zfBJ8HrMZUI.

106. Donald Spoto, *Marilyn Monroe: The Biography* (New York: HarperCollins, 1993), 13.

107. Alan Levy, "A Good Long Look at Myself," in Edward Wagenknecht, ed., *Marilyn Monroe: A Composite View* (Philadelphia: Chilton, 1969), 36.

108. J. Randy Taraborrelli, *The Secret Life of Marilyn Monroe* (New York: Grand Central Publishing, 2009), 391–492; Spoto, *Marilyn Monroe,* 522–98; Keith Badman, *Marilyn Monroe: The Final Years* (New York: Thomas Dunne Books, 2010).

109. Badman, *Marilyn Monroe,* 8.

110. Ibid., 11.

111. Ibid.

112. "I just stuttered," 1960 interview.

113. Spoto, *Marilyn Monroe,* 68; "I just stuttered," 1960 interview.

114. Spoto, *Marilyn Monroe,* 69.

115. The story about the screen test and the name change is in ibid., 110–15.

116. Ibid., 129, 152.

117. Marc Shell, *Stutter* (Cambridge: Harvard University Press, 2005), 159.

118. "Marilyn Monroe," *The Stuttering Foundation,* http://www.stuttering-help.org/famous-people/marilyn-monroe.

119. Spoto, *Marilyn Monroe,* 139.

120. Martin F. Schwartz, "Memoirs of a Stuttering Therapist," http://theflu-encystore.com/memoirs/30_apxa.html.

121. Ibid.

122. Shell, *Stutter,* 141, 288.

123. Ibid., 141.

124. Spoto, *Marilyn Monroe,* 220, 222. Original emphasis.

125. Stanley Buchtal and Bernard Comment, eds., *Marilyn Monroe: Fragments: poems, intimate notes, letters* (New York: Farrar, Straus and Giroux, 2010), 208.

126. Ibid.

127. Wagenknecht, ed., *Marilyn Monroe,* 27.

128. Spoto, *Marilyn Monroe,* 210.

129. Ibid., 225.

130. "I just stuttered," 1960 interview.

131. Francisco Marshall, www.peterrlbrown.blogspot.com.

132. *Augustine of Hippo: A Biography* (1967/2000); *The World of Late Antiquity: AD 150–750* (1971/1989); *The Making of Late Antiquity* (1978); *The Cult of the Saints: Its Rise and Function in Latin Christianity* (1981); *Society & the Holy in Late Antiquity* (1982); "Late Antiquity" ([1985] 1987) in Paul Veyne, ed., *A History of Private Life: 1. From Pagan Rome to Byzantium*; *The Body and Society: Men, Women, and Sexual Renunciation in Early Christianity* (1988); *Power and Persuasion: Towards a Christian Empire* (1992); *Authority and the Sacred: Aspects of the Christianisation of the Roman World* (1995); *The Rise of Western Christendom* (1996/2003); chapters 21 & 22 in *The Cambridge Ancient History, Volume XIII, The Late Empire, A.D. 337–425* (1998); *Poverty and Leadership in the Later Roman Empire* (2002); *Through the Eye of a Needle: Wealth, the Fall of Rome, and the Making of Christianity in the West, 350–550 AD* (2012).

133. Quoted in Francis Oakley, introduction to Peter Brown, "A Life of Learning: the Charles Homer Haskins Lecture for 2003" (American Council of Learned Societies Occasional Paper no. 55, 2003), vii-viii.

134. All the quotations in this chapter, unless otherwise noted, are from a conversation with Dr. Brown at his home in September, 2013.

135. This and all the other quotations in this chapter are from an interview with the author in October, 2013.

136. John Glenn, *John Glenn: A Memoir* (New York: Bantam Books, 1998), 166–67.

137. This and other quotes are from an interview with the author in July 2014.

138. Glenn, *John Glenn*, 50.

139. Glenn, *John Glenn*, 276.

140. Bob Greene, "John Glenn's true hero," *CNN Opinion* (February 20, 2012) http://edition.cnn.com/2012/02/19/opinion/greene-john-annie-glenn.

141. Glenn, *John Glenn*, 326.

142. Ibid., 327.

143. Ibid., 335.

144. Byron Pitts, *Step Out on Nothing: How Faith and Family Helped Me Conquer Life's Challenges* (New York: St. Martin's Press, 2009), 29.

145. Ibid., 25–26.

146. Ibid., 40.

147. Ibid., 41.

148. This and the quotes in the next few paragraphs are from ibid., 43–45.

149. Ibid., 84.

150. Ibid., 74.

151. Ibid., 105–6.

152. Ibid., 129.

153. Interview with author, October 24, 2014.

154. Ibid.

155. *Step Out on Nothing*, 245–46.

156. Personal interview.

157. Ibid.

158. John Updike, "Getting the Words Out," in Updike, *Self-Consciousness: Memoirs* (New York: Alfred A. Knopf, 1989), 80. This essay hereafter will be referred to as GWO.

159. Ibid.

160. Updike, GWO, 87, 83.

161. Ibid., 85.

162. Updike, *Couples* (New York: Alfred A. Knopf, 1968), 52.

163. CBSNews.com staff, "Going Home with John Updike," http://www.cbsnews.com/news/going-home-with-john-updike/.

164. Updike, *Couples*, 200.

165. Adam Gopnik, "Postscript: John Updike", *The New Yorker*, 9 February 2009; Harold Bloom, Introduction, in Bloom, ed., *John Updike: Modern Critical Views* (New York: Chelsea House, 1987), 3; James Wood, "John Updike's

Complacent God," in Wood, *The Broken Estate: Essays on Literature and Belief* (New York: Macmillan, 2000), 192; Updike, *The Early Stories: 1953–1975* (New York: Ballantine Books, 2003), xvii.

166. Updike, *Couples,* 5.

167. Cited in Mary Rourke, "John Updike dies at 76; Pulitzer-winning author," *Los Angeles Times*, 28 January 2009.

168. Cited in Christopher Lehmann-Haupt, "John Updike, a Lyrical Writer of the Middle Class, Dies at 76," *New York Times*, 28 January 2009.

169. Charles McGrath, "Reading Updike's Last Words, Aloud," *New York Times*, 3 April 2009.

170. Updike, "On Being a Self Forever," in *Self-Consciousness*, 230–31.

171. Ibid., 231.

172. Ibid., 230.

173. Adam Begley, *Updike* (New York: Harper-Collins, 2014), 231; Updike, "On Being a Self Forever," 231.

174. David Lodge, "Post-Pill Paradise Lost," in Bloom, *John Updike,* 36; John W. Aldridge, "The Private Vice of John Updike," in Bloom, *John Updike,* 9; Bloom cited in Richard Eder, "The Paris Interviews", *New York Times*, 25 December 2007; Bloom, Introduction, 9; *Literary Review 2008*, http://www.literaryreview.co.uk/badsex_11_08.html.

175. Begley, *Updike,* 210; Updike, "On Being a Self Forever," 222.

176. Updike, "On Being a Self Forever," 250; Begley, *Updike,* 107; Updike, "On Being a Self Forever," 215, 218, 230.

177. Updike, "On Being a Self Forever," 228, 231, 273; Begley, *Updike,* 258.

178. Begley, *Updike,* 224; Updike, GWO, 98.

179. Lodge, "Post-Pill Paradise Lost," 32; Marshall Boswell, "Updike, religion, and the novel of moral debate," in Stacey Olster, ed., *The Cambridge Companion to John Updike* (Cambridge: Cambridge University Press, 2006), 53; Kathleen Verduin, "Updike, women, and mythologized sexuality," in Olster, ed., *The Cambridge Companion*, 68–69.

180. Updike, "On Being a Self Forever," 229, 257, 234; Begley, *Updike,* 197; Frederick Crews cited in Verduin, "Updike, women, and mythologized sexuality," 72.

181. Begley, *Updike,* 482.

182. Updike, GWO, 85, 102.

183. Ibid., 88, 98, 99.

184. Begley, *Updike,* 207, 211; *Couples,* 8.

185. Begley, *Updike,* 328, 409.

186. Ibid., 321, 410.

187. Updike, GWO, 82, 85, 87; Begley, *Updike,* 277.

188. Updike, GWO, 87, 83, 88.

189. CBS interview. See note 6.

190. Updike, GWO, 81.

191. Updike, "On Being a Self Forever," 247.

192. Numbers 12:3.

193. https://en.wikipedia.org/wiki/Norman_Cousins.

194. Proverbs 17:22.

CPSIA information can be obtained
at www.ICGtesting.com
Printed in the USA
LVHW011607160120
643871LV00006B/1117

9 781498 282291